# First World War
## and Army of Occupation
# War Diary
## France, Belgium and Germany

32 DIVISION
Divisional Troops
Northumberland Fusiliers
23 Battalion

WO95/2385/1

The Naval & Military Press Ltd
www.nmarchive.com
Published in association with The National Archives

Published by

## The Naval & Military Press Ltd

Unit 10 Ridgewood Industrial Park,
Uckfield, East Sussex,
TN22 5QE England
Tel: +44 (0) 1825 749494

www.naval-military-press.com
www.nmarchive.com

*This diary has been reprinted in facsimile from the original. Any imperfections are inevitably reproduced and the quality may fall short of modern type and cartographic standards.*

**© Crown Copyright**
**Images reproduced by permission of The National Archives, London, England, 2015.**

# Contents

| Document type | Place/Title | Date From | Date To |
|---|---|---|---|
| Miscellaneous | Personal Account (Possibly By AW Brewin)-No Name in book (First Regt Attached to in France was 23rd Northumberland Fusiliers. | | |
| Miscellaneous | Browne & Nolan, Ltd. Account Book Manufacturers | | |
| Miscellaneous | Joint Council The Order of St. John The British Red Cross Society | 26/02/1931 | 26/02/1931 |
| Miscellaneous | Martins Bank Limited Settle. Yorks. 26th July, 1943 | | |
| Miscellaneous | | | |
| Miscellaneous | B.E.F. | | |

PERSONAL ACCOUNT

(POSSIBLY AW BREWIN) — NO name in title

(FIRST REGT ATTACHED TO IN FRANCE
WAS 23RD NORTHUMBERLAND FUSILIERS

BROWNE & NOLAN, Ltd.
Account Book Manufacturers
No. D9279
Nassau Street, Dublin
WHEN RE-ORDERING PLEASE QUOTE ABOVE NUMBER.

   JOINT COUNCIL

THE ORDER OF ST. JOHN | THE BRITISH RED CROSS SOCIETY

EMERGENCY HELP FUND, ......... DUBLIN CITY BRANCH

14, Merrion Square,
DUBLIN.
26th February, 1931

Marshal & Arran.
I a.m. onbussed to
Averdoingt

Dear Mr. Brewin,

Thank you for your letter. I am so sorry to hear you have had a relapse, and hope you will soon be quite alright again. I will not expect to see you until I hear you are better.

With kind regards,

Yours sincerely,

M. A. Nicholson

2.35 compare watches
4.00 all sleepers moved
5.05 Batt? all ready
5.20 off

6.5 [break time?]
7.20 formed up under barrage
7.36 off

12.15 15" gun [shers?]
9.iv 6 p.m. to Brown Line      Monday

11 p.m. cold rations
                                 Tuesday
10.iv 11 a.m. find a battery
      1 2 5 9
      re-recough 2.f
      Bank laying in 1500 & 2000
                       got
                       away
evening Tynesiders arrive
        sent down for more officers
                              Wednesday
11.iv     A + B. to front line morning
noon   Tynesiders wept after
       also 4th Div a rgt join

11.iv Wednesday [contd]
4.30 Boylers reconnoitre
     ditch 800 to 1000 e.

(Oppy Gavrelle - Fampoux line
                    [shipshap?])

6.30. C + D move into it
      4th Div conform
      Tynesiders day & more
7.15 A + B defensive flank.

12.iv Thursday R.A. Batt? H.Q. Arras
                        at 10 a.m.
                       men the relieved

8.30 p.m. relieved [went bro?]
          by 15th + Lincoln
          sent back to Broad Line

13 iv Friday relieved. lunch at
                               railway
      to Roclincourt valley.

14 iv Sat? slept then
           rendezvoused in
      Lille Rd at 9.20

# MARTINS BANK LIMITED

SETTLE, Yorks.

26th July, 19 43

A. W. Brewin, Esq.,

Eyrefield, Killiney, Co. Dublin.

Dear Mr. Brewin,

I beg to acknowledge receipt of your letter of 13th inst. enclosing cheque amounting to £ 1. 10/- for credit of your account.

I hope you are feeling better.

N

9.4
So we formed a
front along a bit
of the Green Line, &
refused our left
along Tommy Trench
H.Q. remained in
the Brown Line
(he was the 2nd in C.
again)
facing north mostly
10.4
Sat
14th after lunch
S. went over & led
the attack on my own

about 70 killed & missing
& 110 wounded

24th N.F. writing
up war diary
went up on a
lorry from Bavincourt
morning of 28th

3 officers
killed
5 wounded

150 K.W.
M

saw
Stephenson
30th Loot
wife of A officer

at Ratifie la Sagesse des
nations, qui vient de s'asseoir

## B. E. F.

At 11.30 am on Friday 8th Dec. 1916 received Orders to proceed to France for a six weeks course of Instruction as 2nd in Command. I was already awaiting departure on a Cook's Tour (four days in the Line) so was glad of the change, after 14 months at Clipstone. Colonel Tenison (commanding the Reserve Battn) had been offered the Cook's Tour, but, being an 1882 Gyppy Soldier, and some 18 stone in weight, thought the mud would be too much for him, & passed the trip onto me. I was weary of the want of work at Clipstone, having had to chuck up the Adjutancy in April '16, when they discovered I had the august rank of "Temporary Major," & since then had had nothing to do at all, except look after the Mess Morals of the Subalterns.

Some of the 7th Subalterns took all one's time too, seeing that Tenison had had to hold a meeting of Officers in the Mess Room, & instruct them how & where they used the different spoons, forks & knives put before them.

As I was due to cross on the 9th I had to get a move on, & caught the 4 pm train, reached St Pancras 8.30 & so to the Euston where Arthur & Ada were staying.

We yarned after dinner in a drawing room, which I do not suppose had ever had the windows opened, & after lutments I was nearly suffocated.

Arthur & I set out at 10 am & purchasing odds & ends, caught the 11.30 at Charing Cross. Train ordinarily full, leave takings very quiet tho cheery, travelled down with Barker (West Yorks) afterwards badly hit & gassed at Passchendaele, & Goldthorpe who went to a Scottish K. Battalion; both of these were on the same game as I was. The embarking was quick, as ours was the Staff train, the ordinary men of war had had to leave Victoria at 7.30 & to kick their heels round Folkestone until 1 pm when they were allowed on the boat. We sailed as soon as all the Brass Hats were on, only a medium crossing, our escort of three T.B. Destroyers making very heavy weather of it. Staff work at Boulogne execrable – it was pouring with rain, & all new arrivals had to huddle on the quay, in a queue, passing in front of a ticket office window, where half at least of us, were told to report at another office up in Boulogne. No-one knew anything on the quay, & directly disembarkation was complete, all the landing staff disappeared.

I did not wait on the quay, but went & collared a bed at the Louvre Hotel, just outside the station.

It is jolly rough on the Leave Train men who arrive at Boulogne between 8pm & 10pm, & find all beds taken up. When I again arrived on the quay I was sent to the Town Office some half mile up the river, where they told me my destination was the 2nd Army School at WISQUE, the train leaving on a Sunday evening.

Boulogne was very quiet once the Leave Officers had gone, & I wasn't sorry to get into the 4.17. Again no-one could tell me where Wisque was, but as my warrant was endorsed to that place by that train, I had to go.

We meandered along for hours, and I was luckily awake when we reached <u>St Omer</u>, & as I saw no possibility of finding the other place in the dark, I got out there, waited until the train left & then reported to the R.T.O.

I found Wisque was some 5 miles out, so got a fair hotel & bedded down, had a good dinner, & sheets wringing wet. Next morning after breakfast, I chartered a 200 years old cab, & set off; it was deadly cold, snow on the ground, all up hill & we went some four miles an hour.

The destination was a beautiful monastery, on the highest peak of the surrounding country, with a magnificent view, tho' a very dreary one at that time of year.

It was exceedingly cold, no fires in one's rooms, the ante-room was the old chapel, tremendously high & heated with two indifferent stoves, the mess-room was the refectory with no heating apparatus.

70 Officers & 140 N.C.O. were instructed at the school at a time, & there were 7 majors on the same job as myself, who bar one old sportsman were very keen to get back to home & comfort, & were very perturbed when I volunteered that probably those who survived the six weeks, would be commandeered to fill gaps.

The old sportsman was a Col. Lynch, an Irishman in the Scottish Rifles Militia, & he & I foregathered: he was a very good good old chap.

The only amusement was Bridge, & it was really too cold for that, but we had quite a lot amongst ourselves.

On Tuesday we were bundled up to Berthon & Mt. des Cats the former a Trench-mortar school, and the latter a snipers' school.

We travelled in an old London omnibus, all the windows boarded up, & a ground sheet for a door; it was horrid cold, and the roads were frozen & rough, so that it wasn't very much fun, found Keene (Sir John) Commandant of the T.M. School, he was 6 months junior to me at the Shop, and had retired from the Gunners as a captain, so we had a great yarn.

He gave us a very interesting lecture, & then some shooting with them, which (seeing we had only had the prehistoric slings at Clipstone) was good watching.

He said the Boche had much better ones, & were much better at concealing them.

At Mt. des Cats it was Lynch's turn, the Commandant there turning out to be a wild Irishman, who had served with Lynch in peace days: he showed us round all the place, & snipers' plates, armour-piercing bullets, periscope rifles &c., & then would pour whiskey into us. It was very acceptable but when Lynch & he got yarning I thought we never should get away, & nearly offended the old man by insisting on going. We reached Hazebrouck at 7 p.m. fairly chilled, and the gallant majors insisted on staying and having tea !!!!! It was naturally lukewarm & unfit to drink, & we were glad to get home about 9 p.m. Wednesday we watched the officers training: they were very poor compared with Clipstone, & then a Sapper officer with one leg, Greenwood, gave us an excellent exposition of demolition: one, the Bengal torpedo looked excellent, tho' the using of it looked decidedly dangerous. It was some 30 feet long and 2½ inches in diameter (of steel): a party dragged this up to the Bosch wire (if he would allow such a thing) & pushed it under the wire (presumably on a dark night), then cleared off & it was fired by electricity, & blew a gap some 10 to 15 yards wide in the wire. It certainly did its job excellently. We received our orders that night to go to different divisions for the rest of the six weeks: I think they were bored stiff at Wisque finding us anything to do.

The adjutant was exceedingly nice (a Welsh Guardsman) & gave us a list of the Divisions we were to be allotted to, so that any with friends could go near them. All the lot had considerable wind up except Lynch, who oddly enough was sent home in February as too old (I met him at Boulogne as I came back from leave: he was very downcast). Two of us reported to the 34th Division. We drove to St. Omer, trained to Hazebrouck, & from there in a car to Croix-du-Bac. From there I went to the 102nd Brigade H.Q. at Erquinghem whilst my companion went to the 103rd Brigade. I was attached to the 23rd N.F. (4th Tyneside Scottish) & joined them at the village.

they were out of the Line, the 101st & 103rd were in the Line, a two-battalion frontage, one Battⁿ of each in Front Line, one in Close Support, one in Reserve, and one in Erquinghem. Porch, the C.O. was home on sick leave: he was an East Surrey Dug Out (a contemporary of Vic Birkbeck whom he knew very well), a very stalwart man. Longhurst was 2nd in Command, a little bow-legged newsagent from Newcastle. How he had got there I don't know, except that the 34th had got a horrid hammering at La Boisselle near Albert, on the 1st July 1916. They had no tact in those days and everyone except the Quartermaster and Transport Officer went over the top: the C.O., 2nd in Command, Adjutant, Assistant Adjt., Signalling Officer, all Company Sergeant Majors, Company Quartermaster Sergeants, down to the last man bugler. As a result there was nothing to start off again with & Longhurst (then a captain) & two subalterns were all that were left. The Division had never recovered from the Somme; the 102nd & 103rd had both been practically wiped out; the 101st were luckier & were decidedly good, but the 102nd & 103rd had never got good recruits since & suffered accordingly.

The country & roads were I should say, typically Flanders like, very heavy holding ground, great dykes, and the roads paved, with cart space on each side in the mud.

On Saturday 16th. I rode to Armentières with Coull (a Company Commander & liaised with an Australian Brigade which was to be on our left during our next trip in the line. Armentières was not badly knocked about, & had some fine buildings, business going on more or less as usual, shops & cafés open. The cathedral was badly broken, and of course some houses, & the east side was wrecked, but the Boch apparently was willing to let live, seeing that

11

some gunners had their H.Q. in an eastern suburb, from the windows of which you could see all the Aubers ridge with the Bosch trenches &c. The railway station was badly bent too, & from there we went along a long communication trench to the Australian Battn. H.Q. in a big farm in the open, only 400 yards behind the front line. No one appeared to worry about protection, probably because the whole country was waterlogged, and digging impossible. The same Australians were also very casual, & the H.Q. was like a bee-hive; everyone appeared to stroll in across the open, & didn't care at all that the Bosch was watching everything from the ridge opposite. They got out alright, but the unfortunate people some months afterwards, found themselves the target of a concentrated shoot, and the farm was wiped off the map. I found that was the usual spirit tho', people saying "Oh we are going out to-morrow", & caring little for their poor reliefs.

The 2ⁿᵈ in Command took us round, & as it was my first experience of Australians in France, I found it quite interesting. Their trenches were not clean by any means, & they showed great tendency to bunch together, to talk &c, & apparently their men were not compelled to rest, as in our lines, but as it was their first effort, it was not so bad. They had had a poor start on their first day, thro' this same bunching: the Bosch put some Meinenwerfers over (in future called minnies — or trench-mortars) & the Australians stood in groups & watched them coming, & were greatly surprised when one pitched amongst a group of ten of them, & wiped the lot out.

The Bosch was some 300 yards away, so we could have a good look at things over the top. Being my first time in the front line I had to do it, tho' feeling very peevish about it, ignorance suggesting that there was a man aiming straight at the spot, waiting for you to put your head over. It was very muddy & the only shelters were in the traverses, which only gave some six inches overhead cover, and a three foot six high cupboard. We came out to Armentières for lunch, & I was greatly surprised to find an excellent feed, hors d'oeuvres &c, fish, entrée, joint & sweets, & very reasonable prices, with stout, beer or whiskey. As the feeding at Erquinghem was not luxurious we made the most of it.

The 18th Coull & I rode to Estaires, a very old & old-fashioned Flanders country market town: we were in search of turkeys, but naturally all had been bought up: got a hair-cut & feed, & so back. The roads were very muddy, & in bad repair, not pavé, very like the old white limestone Settle roads after continuous rains.

On the 20th I saw the first sausage balloon, & my first Bosch aeroplane. We were going round the encampment when he came over quite low: the mob showed their discipline by all dashing out of their bivouacs & gazing at him, never thinking of shooting (the Routine Orders being that no man leaves cover, & all those in the open stay exactly where they are, leaving the Lewis guns & guards to shoot). He came back again directly after very close down, & not a shot was fired, so he got a cheap ride. The next day we had the Regimental Christmas dinner for the Officers. Usually the Company officers have Company messes, and the C.O., 2nd in Command, Adjutant, Assistant Adjt., Signalling Officer, intelligence officer and doctor form a H.Q. mess. We gathered everyone tho' for this night, & held it at H.Q. mess. It was an excellent dinner, & we had a very cheery evening.

On the 22nd, Haig came to inspect the Brigade. It was an awful wet day, & there not being a field big or dry enough for us, he saw them march past on the road. I was not included, & as he took the salute from just opposite the H.Q. mess I had a good view, & was not greatly struck. The gunners were the best & cleanest, our battalion (Tyneside Scottish) were piggy dirty & had made no effort to get rid of the mud from the last tour in the line.

We went into the line the next day, relieving the 1st Tyneside Irish at Chapelle Armentières, just S.E. of Armentieres. The march in was very funny & was more like a fair than anything else: everyone marched straight down the middle of the road, or rather slouched down it, right to the end of the communication trench just by the chapel. Those coming out were just as careless, & as the Bosch looked right down upon us from the Aubers ridge, it seemed like looking for trouble; nothing did happen though, & I found out afterwards (at least it was the only explanation I could make fit) that it was a case of "Live and let live": we didn't worry them when we saw anything, & he did ditto. First there were the Gunner O.P.'s; in our battalion sector there were only two possible places for O.P., close to the line, two farm buildings, one on each side of B.H.Q., & these were constantly used by the gunners; they certainly got a few shells through them, but as one was a Strong Point, & H.Q. of a Company, the movement around it would naturally make the Bosch send some over as a warning to keep quiet. Then in a morning, all Co. H.Q.'s could be picked out by a feather of smoke arising therefrom, due to the fact that the cook was too lazy to get up in the dark and light his bucket brazier & get the charcoal red hot & all the wood burnt up before daylight (seeing that B.H.Q. was just as careless they probably thought they were justified), & it gave one a very safe idea of trenches, an opinion one had sadly to revise when we moved down south. The discipline of the Tynesiders was pretty awful, & Longhurst was the last

I went round the line with Longhurst one day; there were a few shells dropping about, & when we got to the junction of Cowgate, the Communication Trench, and the front line, L. paused & looked around to see which direction it seemed safest to go in. A shell dropped over about 50 yards on our right, so he set off to the left; another dropped over about another 50 yards in front of us. L. stopped; I pushed along, for one looked such a fool; another came over in the same place, and I heard a voice from one of the shelters say in a contemptuous voice:—"Heigh, there goes t' bow-legged little beggar, running away again!" I looked back, & just saw L. disappearing full tilt down Cowgate!!

man to have even temporary command of a slack lot. I know Porch told me, later on, before I left him, that he always found it desperately hard to pick up the threads again after he had been away, as no one took any notice of Longhurst, & the latter hadn't the slightest idea <u>how</u> to set about making himself obeyed.

The weather was not so ghastly as we went on, but grey & misty & the trenches were very wet. B.H.Q. a very comfy breastwork was on the banks of a stream running parallel to our lines, & this used to flood quite often, so that it was never what you would call dry. At the H.Q. I found one of the majors who had come out with me, & in fact the one who came to the 34th Div'n: he gave a most dismal tale of his life, said he'd never had his boots off all the tour, & he had five days whiskers on him, so had not enjoyed life much: at the end of his six weeks he was not recommended by the C.O. to whom he was attached as fit to go as 2nd in Command to a Batt'n, & they posted him as a Company Commander. I was always sorry for the company he had, & later I heard that the prospects of an April offensive were too much for him, & he retired from the line, (to I suppose a nice soft job behind).

The B.H.Q. was quite comfy cosy to what I had expected, two rooms, one the C.O.'s retiring room, & the other the H.Q. mess, only 18 inches below ground level, windows facing out to the back, & a fireplace in one corner for burning coke, & we were very nearly suffocated by night time by the fumes, but it was beautifully warm so what matter. The adjutant & his assistant had a small similar place a little further along, & the signal officer & staff were in cubby-holes all down the bank; the doctor had his Aid Post some 50x away quite a nice airy place, two entrances, & a small room for sleeping in. There was tremendous congestion until we chased out the relieved H.Q. which happened on the signal being sent in from the slowest company that all in their company sector was O.K. Then Longhurst & I went round the line. We were a particularly compact Rectangle of Occupation, & one couldn't lose one's way, though woe betide you if you slipped off the duckboards in the front line. The whole show was breastwork & they had taken the soil (or mud) to fill the sandbags from just behind, never leaving even space for a pathway, in consequence of which there was a great lagoon just behind the front line, & the duckboards were laid on piles driven into the mud; & when the floods rose & the winds blew, the said duckboards were under water, & you had to feel your way along. It was an awful do at night, & not being able to see at all by night I found it very slow.

My shelter was a very dank & drear place, also on the edge of the stream, not high enough to stand up in but as I only slept shaved & washed there it didn't matter, & anyway the third night the water rose & I found six inches of water on the floor, so after that I slept on a stretcher in the mess, & very cosy too.

We had a very comfy. evening the first night; I found a Piquet player in Coull (who was acting 2nd in Command & so attached to H.Q.) so we had a good time, & I did not chance my arm round the line in the dark. Next morning I went round at dawn to see the ceremony of <u>stand down</u>. The men were horribly comfortless; they spent all night in the Fire Bays on the Fire Step; certainly they were fairly dry under foot, but in the daytime they snuggled in shelters just behind the bays, some three feet high & six feet long, no shell-proof cover, open towards the rear, overlooking the lagoon — not very pleasant in the cold & wet, & the shelters were always falling in, with damp & concussion. They changed their socks & rubbed feet at stand-down,

20

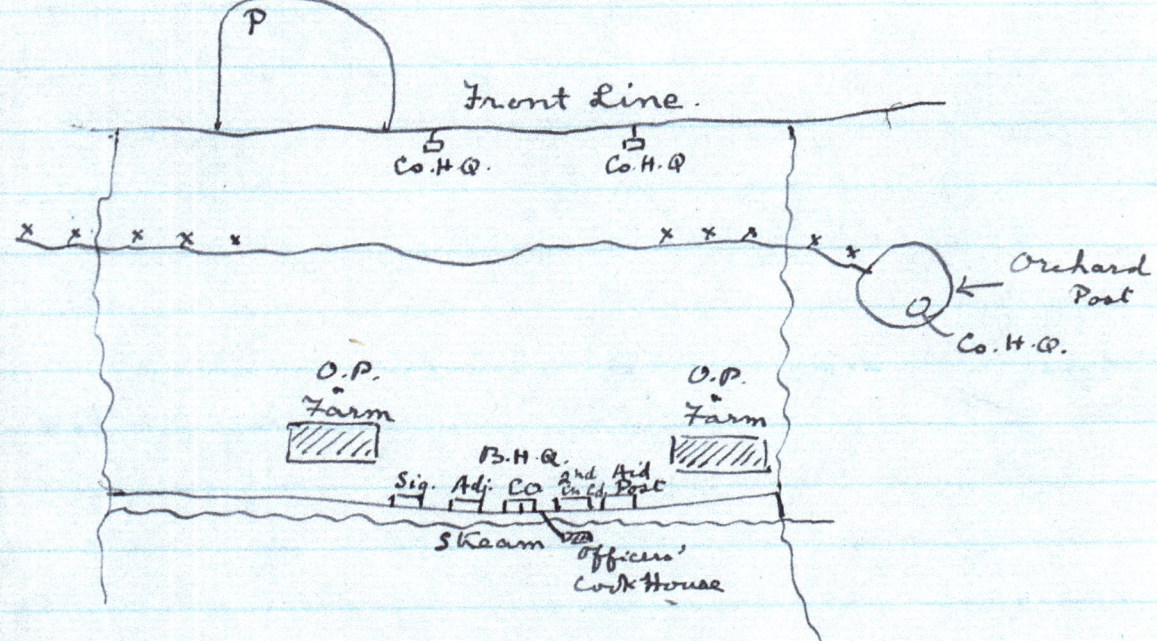

& were supposed to shave, but they were very slack about the latter, & the officers were not well shaven either. Their Company H.Q.s were pretty deadly, only 5 ft. high at the most, & no shell cover. One Co. H.Q. caught a direct hit from a 4.5 about a month ago & killed all five officers there. I think though it was a chance shot for the Bosch (as I said before) must have known the exact position of each.

The line was held only in parts, owing to the bad state of the breastworks, a bay or two every 20 or 30 yards; two companies in the front line & two in support as shown opposite. Chard's Farm, (the house had been in the centre, but nothing was left, and the rectangle was the old paddock line, & had had poplars all around. It was awfully wet & blown about, just a line of breastwork around the paddock, a bit trenched as well, & as a stream ran in from the Bosch line at P, & they stood higher than we did, he used to pump his trenches down this stream into our line. We had a pump at Q & used to push it off towards the Australians, (when our pump worked, which was seldom, & when I was there the pump was under water! Chard's Farm was awfully wet, & no picnic to visit either by day or night. The Bosch minnied it most unmercifully & it looked like nothing on earth - just a heap of mud & tree stumps. Between us & the Australians was a gap of 200ᵡ with no defence; this gap was patrolled by night from end to end, but the Bosch must have been very slow, or he would have had a real good raid there bang up to B.H.Q. It was a bad bit of defence.

Coull was with me on all my explorations, a good officer & most helpful, as Scotch as they make them: he finally got a job under the Admiralty at home. I was very lucky in getting him for he put me up to what were legitimate & illegitimate risks, & what was done & what was not

22

Langhurst poor chap, dodged all the Shows in '17, & finally got a job at the Dep't at Newcastle, I have no doubt the strain of constant windiness broke him up just as easily as anything else, & after a fortnight at Newcastle he was killed in a motor cycle accident, so didn't gain much.

done: he had a whole hearted contempt for Longhurst, & from I pieced together the latter had shown up very badly in rough houses. It is extraordinary how wrong one's ideas (formed before going into the line) are, & I had to remodel most of mine, seeing that things I thought safe were distinctly otherwise, & things I thought risky were everyday occurrences & were thought nothing of.

Christmas Eve was quite nice & sunny, & with a certain amount of care, and luck in not sliding off greasy duck-boards, one got fairly dried. One is more or less wet-footed all the time in the line, as it is impossible to avoid deep mud & water in the dark, but the clean sock stunt was a great help, although the heart-breaking strain of struggling into wet boots took a lot out of one, & it would have been very nice to let things slide.

The food management for the men was very poor: they got no hot food during their five days tour in the front line, and not even hot tea. It was purely bad organization, & I found out later what could be done in that line with capable organization. The breastworks & water stopped all idea of dug-outs, but they were building "Baby Elephants" before we left. These are Concrete Pill Boxes, over very strong ribbed ironwork, sunk as far as the water allows; generally this had been misjudged & the water was anything up to two feet deep in the interior.

There was some shelling during the afternoon, & towards dusk they sent over some minnies, most terrifying things, & making craters anything to 10 yards across. (I smile when I read this & think of the Gwenchy minnies which did twice the damage & really did alter the landscape. The sentries are told off to warn folks of their arrival, but they are bad judges of direction, & when they shouted "minnie left" it was safer to locate it before scampering forever; you can see them coming quite easily, & often can hear the click of discharge, rather like a bolt being re-loaded in a rifle with no cartridge in. The minnies look like knobberries as they have round heads & a tail about to steady it. With care one can judge pretty ac-curately where they will land & so move off to safer places, but at night time they are the devil; you can see them then by a stream of red sparks, looking about 2ft long, passing across the sky, & the Boosh looses off about four or five together, seeing there is no chance of our locating the firing positions by night. & you can see trails of sparks crossing one another, till you don't know which way to run, & finally your itty is a bad job & sit-tight.

Not afternoon a subaltern had his trench coat spread out on the parapet to dry, & a minnie burst some 20 yards away, after which there wasn't a sign of the coat to be found. Of course one gets compensation sooner or later, but you first have to write a report of the thing. The C.O. has to certify that the lad hasn't destroyed it, the bill for the coat to be attached to the reports, & a certificate from Cox to say the coat hasn't wandered into his "Officers kit" department; it's an awful shame, & the delay may be anything up to six months.

The method of dealing with Boosh advisory late shelling was ridiculous, & as follows. Supposing the Boosh shelled a certain sector of our front line, the com-pany concerned phoned to B.H.Q., the C.O. telephoned to the gunners, & the gunners loophed up their retaliation table, & shelled a certain part of the Boosh line, not necessarily opposite to where he was shelling. Then it became a case of who cared in front & finally the man ended by no sector giving in & phoning the

gunners & denied, after which the whole thing died away.
It was a prehistoric method, & I had heated arguments with the Tyrenidiers over it, saying it was a childish & a lazy way out of the difficulty. I later introduced my plan at Guerchy (Heavens! in 1918 if you please!). It was for the Company Commander to be able to get through fire to the gunners without B.H.Q. butting in & wasting time; the gunners knew many of the Bosch battery positions, & was assisted by company commanders who reported to the gunners; the direction from which the shelling was coming; the size of the shell; any other information, & the severity or otherwise of the same. The gunners were very keen on it, & brought me to their maps, & one used to spend hours locating battery positions, & so smoothly did my company work with them, that I reduced the whole thing to two letters, one letter representing supposed Bosch battery in action, & the other whether severe or otherwise. I got splendid support from the gunners who lived pounding the Bosch. It created awful jealousy at A.H.Q. though. Jo they were cut out of the show altogether, & rated a mere company commander running a gun do. At Guerchy my men were greatly interested in it, & had direction sticks all along the line, & with great pride used to report a Bosch battery or gun of 4.5" in this direction, Sir: "Hadn't produce our gun map, & we'd check, & they were ryt. be awfully pleased if they were ryt.
The Road at Armentières naturally didn't care two pence if his infantry were getting shelled, so long as he could prevent our firing with impunity.
Christmas Day was started with a steady shelling over part just to tell the Road that there was no fraternizing this year, but it died about 9 a.m. &

nothing happened until 2 a.m. when he put over a few 5.9mm's. He kept shelling a bit until dusk. I went round the line with Longhurst about 10 a.m. The discipline was bad, trenches were dirty with tins & scattered about, men unshaven & dirty, & rifles ditto, quite contrary to what we had been taught at home, & to what I saw in other units. The men were consequently the biggest sufferers & got awfully smashed up at La Boiselle on July 1st 1916. Out of all their experienced officers & men & the lads who had succeeded as company commanders were very poor imitations.

Boxing Day was very foggy. to I amused myself wandering about on top, between the front & support lines, & picking up odds & ends. A few minnies came over from the village of Wez Macquart, just opposite, in the afternoon, but very nearly all day Claud's farm is the favourite hunting ground for minnies, & they've made a most hopeless mess of it. The authorities unfortunately set great store by Claud's farm, tho' only I, tho' didn't evacuate it, & put the front line behind it. I never knew. As it was, when firing started everyone used to clear out except two Lewis Gun teams, one at each corner, & if there had been an attack, everything would have been just the same as if they had never told it, & they could have wired the Lewis guns well in & lived happily further back. As it is, the line gets blown in & then the flimsy rise & you stand in anything up to 4ft of water with no shelters, & merely in at right a perfect nightmare with new roles & derivations everywhere. I remember going round one day, & they had blown the a bit of the trench right in, & the only way was to scramble over the top of the pile of mud & down the other side. I puncked up &, on top, got landed on to some buried wire & couldn't shift either way, & I was in full view of the Board Car & big fragment. I felt very faded & was jolly glad I ordered something - gave a pilot down under cover.

We went into support on the 27th. The relief took 5 hours to complete, an awful show, what it would be like relieving at night with the Btn, I shudder to think. Our B.H.Q. was a deserted farm on a road leading from Chapelle Armentières, about a mile from the line, & there we got warmed & dried & loaded & bathed. I had an excellent one with the Gunners, whose H.Q. was in a house with a bathroom & geyser complete. N.B., part, your batman carries a towel kit into the line, feeling (in a waterproof sheet), a blanket, socks, washing things, etc, and the transport brings up your kit when you are in support or reserve.

On the 29th, Herm (one of Caulli's subs), and I went to Bailleul by bus, a ride of I french hour, untroubled, with a big square & a fair officers' club, just off it, & had a fair dinner, made a few purchases, & got back again by 10p.m.

We went into the line, Rou?jean's Sue, found the floods out, & everything shocking wet & not amusement bothering men slip off duckboards, until one does it one's self. The Boche was very angry & sent over 179 minnies between 2 & 4 p.m., & never a casualty, mad extraordinary, though the line was badly bent, & poor Chand's farm was in an awful state. I went round it next day; you've never seen such a lot of debris, tiles, wire, duckboards, mud & water, it as the tides were choked, the water was well up to one's waist awfully cold! Besides which, one was fully exposed to the view of the Boch, & his snipers were quite busy, just when we wanted to hurry over a bad bit, one would be tied up in a barbed wire.

When I got back to B.H.Q. I found King there, he is a subaltern of gunners, & served in the South African war, so we had a great yarn. He had fired a salvo from his battery at maximum elevation at midnight on New Year's Eve, to some innocent folks miles behind the line must have been a bit astonished. There (was) yarn he told me, which was amusing, & which oddly enough I saw in print after the war. I was about a gunner Forward Observation Officer. He is tacked on to the guns by a telephone wire run out, & observes the shooting, & sends back the necessary corrections which he observes as necessary. It arose out of some Company Commander in B? Commander ('Fred' which) remarking that it was a pity the Gunners could not compare the man of the Infantry of their powers to shoot accurately. The Gunner Major who was there, he met struck with the idea and offered to arrange a shoot shoot at that sector of the line, & they agreed that Wig. Kneppert church tower would be O.K., as it could be seen from the whole of the Batt? frontage, & all Co. Commanders were told to mistrust their men as to the target, which was the clock face on the tower of the church, which faces our line. The Gunner Forward Observing Officer was about 150 yards in front of our BHQ in a steel hive they had put up. This was an exact imitation of a real hive, the top of which had been blown off by a shell, & the real hive had been cut down one night, & the imitation put up, with of course a ladder up the inside, and an observing slit cut in front just below the top.

The procedure is for the F.O.O. to be up top, the telephone operator & instrument at the bottom, all in functions being repeated by the telephone operator before being relayed to the guns. The guns fired first, hit the target tower from a 10ft. below the clock, & with a correction given for elevation, the second, as hit the edge of the face, & all the others (they fired fifteen) were either on the face, or very close to, & all hit the tower, excepting one round somewhere in the middle of the tower which was some 300 yards short. The infantry were greatly impressed with the shoot, & of course it tickled them up no end to know that Gunners could shoot so perfectly they were Whizz Bangs on Field Guns — but the odd party it was him. The position of the interested persons were as opposite. After the second shot, there was practically no need of correcting but of course the range & direction for each ensuing shot was called out by the F.O.O. & phoned to the guns by the operator. Thus if the second shot was phoned as 2600 yards line correct, and 30 ft. afterwards would be similar, unless the round fell low or high, & the amount lower or high would be judged by the F.O.O. & a correction of range would be sent by him to tell the guns where the last shell fell.

The infantry meanwhile were greatly amused by a Boyish sportsman in the front line at A who evidently saw what was on, & signalled across (showing himself to do so) in the same manner as a marker in rifle butts would signal to those at the firing point. He did it with a shovel, & a dug out was standing up behind him, or some elevated piece of earth — if a shell hit the face he would place the blade of his shovel straight on the centre of this elevation; if quite close to, he would point his shovel up & down once or twice, & then first the blade of his shovel on the approximate spot of his target corresponding to the part of the tower hit; if not near the face, he would swing his shovel over his head back & forwards & then plant it in a spot similar to that hit. This greatly

Lug Inaguart          Boyrch Front Line
Church

        A
        o

                British Front Line


F.O.O.     o Road Face
Inn.  o           o

          o B-HQ          o British Guns.

amused the British spectators; however about the middle of the shoot, one shell fell short & hit A, However the unfortunate Boach & 5 mitrailleurs. When the F.O.O. was in BHQ after the shoot, the infantry remonstrated with him for killing a sportsman, but said that that had improved the moral more than anything. The F.O.O. was completely puzzled & denied shooting anyone, but said one shell fell extraordinarily short, & that he had treated it as a freak; he could not see where it dropped as a real tree was in his line. The infantry then got puzzled & told him about the Boach marker. "Bone puzzled! So the telephone operator was sent for. "Oh yes, he said" "remember that round very well" ("Le of course could see nothing, either good or bad") "& was puzzled why you gave me 2200 instead of 2800" — "I never did," said the F.O.O. So then they rang up the guns & asked for the ranges of the shoot, & sure enough, there was one round 2200 & the others all 2800 or approximately so. The half of this 600 yards would have lodged a shell at the foot of the tower, and the other half caused it to fall 300* short at A (the figures of course are not the correct ones). Well they never made it out. The F.O.O. swore he never gave that reduction in range; the operator swore he did & that moreover he had asked for a "Repeat" of the order, & that still the F.O.O. called down the data. The infantry had seen the results, & the unfortunate Boach was the victim of a most extraordinary accident.

They have a new amusement just now at B.H.Q. The officers cook performs his duties in a shanty of corrugated iron, and every half hour or so some sportsman sniffs to a with a big rock, aimed at it with knocker from the iron buildings, & hurls it at the shanty, cuts open the cork, fearfully scared: he never failed to "bob".

On the 2nd, the gunners did a 10 minutes "Hurricane Bombardment" on a supposed meeting place of Boch. I watched it from the O.P. + was greatly impressed. I notice in my diary I wrote "10 minutes Hell" [well nowadays] I fear one would think very little of it. — in the retaliation the C.O. nearly caught a "sig" to our own trench mortars had some marvellous escapes from sunnies — evidently they had had their position spotted, + hurriedly shifted their pitches during the night. The C.O. arrived hew year's Day — an awfully nice chap, but told nothing but shop — from dawn till dark — most interesting for me but H.Q. joyfully bored. Cuill tried a daring feat on the 3rd, being an engineer, to drain Chard's Farm, but he went astray, + flooded the draining pump deeper than it has ever been before !

On the 4th we went to reserve in the outskirts of Armentieres, quite nice, baths on. + then Longhurst Cuill + I went to dine at Lucienne's, a supposed spy — found excellent. The lady most charming, surprised me by telling me that she hadn't seen me there since my regiment was Here in April 1915 !! good effort, eh ?

The next few days were attacked to a 60 pounder battery in front of Erquinghem, but it was very foggy + not much shooting done; but they put me wise as to map shooting, + the new corrections made for damp, barometer, errors of gun etc. very interesting. The men have a rotten time in reserve, as they are on working parties all night + every night, which seems wrong.

Then we went in again to the front line. One day there was great preparations as the Brigadier was coming up to go round the line. Roach (the C.O.) Longhurst + I were waiting for him at the top of little road, where it joins the front line, but after wasting an hour or having a pretty hot time dodging Boche shells, which were falling thick & fast round our rendezvous, all we got was a runner with a note saying that the Brigadier had been called to Div S.H.Q. — an awful lie we found out afterwards — he had got within 200 yards of us & then funked the shelling. He was an awful ass, & was sent home after the Arras show on Easter Monday '17.

On the 10th we had an funny do. The C.O. & I went out & saw the Brigadier. At the bottom of the C.T. instead of going along the reserve line and the usual way, the C.O. clambered out & went across some exceptionally muddy fields. I was very annoyed, but rather pleased when about four whizzbangs burst in the reserve trench just about where we should have been! The C.O. said he couldn't tell what made him go that way, as he had never been before.

On the night of the 10th, I spent it with Cradell who was with his company shooting at the Boche wire. You can see the sparks when successful — firing very light r. c. I had a big cantur No Man's Land — lovely broonlight & full of wire — a beautiful night, but I was home before morning from Co. H.Q. not a patch on B.H.Q. for comfort!

On the 11th was a general Court Martial at Ervillers. The Brigadier was president, & afterwards he & we had in his car, & lunched with him. Excellent cigar afterwards — an amusing old thing but full of stuff. Home snow at night, a very cold.

We went out in rain in serpent, & in the weather was vile. I spent my time going over the correspondence files. I got quite a lot of this, & read an awful lot of rubbish. We had had frost & snow till we went out to rest at Ervillers.

Pooh, as I said, was awfully 'shoppy', & could neither talk nor think anything but 'shop' all day long. He used to sit for minutes together with his elbows on the table & hands over his face, & then draw his hands down till his face was cupped in his hands, and propound some awful conundrum about the raid, or the line. One got bored stiff with shop, & we used to flee out & leave him. He got on so on to one's nerves, & one would much rather be 'going round to the Co. H.Q"s', & chatting with the company officers, than enduring continual 'shop'.

One day I was made prosecutor on a Court-Martial on a man of the Tynesiders, who was up for being found of Boulogne when he ought to have been in the front line. It was a most unusual thing, for the prosecutor is either the Adjutant on Court-Adjutant. I asked Ponsonby I had been put on, & he told me it was at the Brigadier's special request; he imagined I should have more ideas, being an old Soldier, of the enormity of the offence, and that I could impress the Court to that effect!!! Heavens! I know amused I was, for beyond prosing him

It was brightly cold there, bright frost & brown showers. I spent my time getting her old correspondence filed. I had one or two in Comines, but otherwise kept the fire warm & ranked my stars that I was not in the line. We were preparing a big battalion raid for Cats on, to be done the next town. The ground was most unsuitable. I never thought much of it, but the brigadier was very keen, & Brock also. But he hadn't had any fear too kind, & they had exploded up & down with machine guns & strong points. I was glad I wasn't going. R.H. Lott the C.O. went down to the line to study the actual ground. Lots of fog in Comines, the idea would have been to some time didn't. I made a huge noise when we went through! We located all the lines of advance we proposed using, mostly ditches & not at that, & next day we rehearsed the raid on ground just so looked out to represent the place. Each company is lending 2 officers & 20 men.

On the 22nd I went on leave. Of course the trains never turned up until late, & we heard no chance of a gallop to Steenwerck, where I entrained at 3 a.m. We crawled down via Hazebrouck & St. Omer, & arrived at Boulogne. Starved & frozen at 9.20. Had a huge feed. They only had omelets & cold ham, so we devoured cold ham while they cooked omelets, & had three courses of each. I slept in the smoking room at the Louvre Hotel, just opposite the station. The hotel of course was crammed, we however got beds in the smoke room, & after supper, on retiring there, we found some spinsters had booked the same quarters. We got the manageress, & on opening the door in there I saw six old dames in their beds, but cleared them out & slept comfily. It was cold & wet next morning & we an easy gay crossing, but it was the right way, & the boat left at 10 a.m. Arrived Folkestone 11.45. Town train 1.30, in plenty of time to find Co'l! & Lang posted myself

---

Said, "you are supposed to leave everything else to the Court, & he should have made me president of the Court, as the man who can swing the members to rubbing it in, on lenency."

I heard afterwards from the Bde Major that Trevor-Jean, on the brigadier, had said that no one had been a shot in the brigade yet, & that he thought it would have a very bracing effect on the men, if they did shoot some one, & this unfortunate lad was to be the scapegoat. As a matter of fact the lad was half daft, & had been on leave, & on coming back, was told he was transferred to another Tyneside batt'n. He wouldn't it, & they would have none of it, nor would his old battalion, nor did they, as they reasonably might have done. Rely Lem, but just-told him to go & be damned! So he wandered off & having no home or anything, meandered off down the line, & found himself at Boulogne, where he attached himself to different units to get food &c. & was finally, copped & sent back. Needless to say, the g.c.m.j. & Jerman was bitterly disappointed!

out with india rubber cont. boilers, & sent off my borrowed kit to Long Vt. I caught the 11.30 train from Euston & breakfasted at the County Hotel, Lancaster. (Strachan Campbell was there. I knew him when he was a major at Malta in 1895: he commanded the Weston Division, & with rather bad luck got sacked over the Connollis West case). Detrained all morning, & to Clapham at 3.30 p.m. Left Clapham on Feb 1st. I had put in for extra leave to get my teeth settled, & though I wired several times could learn nothing from the War Office, & at 5 p.m. on the day I left they received a wire at Clapham saying I was granted a week's extension.

Had a very comfy trip to Boulogne, & was under[way] for the midnight train. We left punctually enough in a cold stone train, & two miles outside stood fast until 3 a.m., finally arrived at St Omer at 8.20, so gave up & cleared out of the train; my feet were so frozen that I could not feel them, & indeed I didn't get complete judging-power for several days. It was about as cold a night as I have known. So I went to a hotel to get breakfast & a good warm, & on again about 11 a.m. in a Leff gr. train, picked up the Batt? at a place called Godewaersvelde just under Mt des Cats. Quite good billets. No 'cold', nothing to do, so kept the fires warm. The C.O. was still at Armentières with the raiding party, as the raid had been postponed. Went into Ruilbel one day by bus to learn a gunner before on "Artillery on the Somme"; a very poor do. The weather was bright & snowy, but most infernally cold; one morning my teeth were frozen solid in the glass. I had to take them to bed with me to thaw them out. I had a bedroom about 40 feet square (& high) & it was poisonously cold dressing. At No 80 we had a Brigade route march. The organization was horrid, the Batt? being kept standing on Loos in a very cold wind with the temperature down towards Zero. I didn't want to get sick in that brigade.

Next day I was ordered to join the 16th Royal Scots at Renton as 2nd in Command, so walked over Mt. des Cats & down to Berthen. The C.O., Stephenson, came from Rhodesia, an awfully good chap — had originally been commissioned in the K.O.Y.L.I., & was at Loos with them in one of those unfortunate divisions which marched 20 odd miles & then straight into the scrap with packs on, no rations, & no one knew where they were or where they were going to. Their general objective was Douai! There were no reserves & they broke over from the 1st Division who had done quite well. The Bosch came out these lads straight through, whollered them & booked them, then broke through their flank & attacked them from the rear, so they had to go & lost all the ground won by the 1st.

He was with the 16th R.S. on the Somme in '16, & his brigade, 101, was in reserve. The 10 2nd Tyneside Scottish went over first, on the left fully of La Boiseille, they were nI (& never will be) Thurston, & never reached the Bosch wire, but lost heavily in Officers, the Tyneside Irish in support came yards behind the slopes over the top, but very few reached our original front line. Poor Howard, ( in the Natal Police with me) commanded the 24th N.F., & was killed just in front of our front line; he was badly wounded, & four men were killed trying to get him in, so he had to be left till dark, & died that night — altogether a bad show. Apparently the Bosch defended us by his machine guns, which were untouched by our shelling.

On Saturday the 10th, the C.O. took me round the billets. Berthen lies in a hollow right under the hill, the cold, so we were pretty cosy but the weather was desperate cold. We were in outlying farms, H&Q & A Company at one big farm, B, C, & D about ½ mile away at others. The billets were quite good; I slept in a very comfy bed in the same room as the C.O., & he used to yarn no end, quite different from Ponsonby though who invariably talked shop. He told me a good yarn of a bad show in Sept.r 1916. He was 2nd in Command & two companies were going over at dawn. The C.O., an extraordinary old Stirling£ gentleman, Sir George McCrea, was in bed, & not even interested enough to find out how things were going. Stephenson was on the phone, but could not get no news, so left an hour after Zero, rushed down to the front line & found chaos. The two companies were all over the place, mixed in with the garrison of the line, & a hopeless mess. Apparently the company commanders hadn't got their men down in time, & the barrage had come & gone before they were ready. He got on to brigade, & the brigadier ordered the attack to be made at once (very easy to say); there was no barrage, it was broad daylight, and the Bosch had noted all the mix up in the line & was all ready for them; both company commanders were killed, & the companies lost heavily. Sir George was sent home, & Stephenson got the Batt.n He now wears a fine lot, & the Bffurs well deserve the average, & very cheery, a nice thing to see, as there is evidently "dirty work at the Cross Roads" due in the spring.

 11th. Hauled off & on the next few days; the ground was frozen a foot deep though, & the only result was a surface of 3 lines under a few inches of water. We practiced over spring shown, ploughed out ground, very difficult to imagine, & very funny to watch. They got lined up & getting ahead in the back after having moved over a trench. & how special platoons are told off to each bit of captured trench. They are called "moppers up", which explains itself. The general formation for attack, as worked out by our G.S. work staff officers during the winter, is as opposite. It gives one a comfy feeling, knowing that moppers up are busy, as you push along to another line, knowing all your troubles are in front. We buried the practice with condemnates. It was awfully hard keeping formation on the ice-bound roads.

We were very unfortunate in having a very cold room for H.Q. mess. A. Co. had the kitchen & were nice & warm. The stove being in beautiful order & always going full blast. Still they were very pleasant days, & even bedroom was as warm as anything, being next to the kitchen.

You have a good view of Ypres from the tops of the hills & on a clear day you can see the sea ( the same way in which you see the Isle of Man from Scafell). I've never seen it on that anyone who had, but the view is beautiful.

On the 18th Feb.? it took up again & froze hard, & the going was like glass, as it was mostly up hill and down dale, you can imagine what hard work it was. We suffered from bad brigade orders, often during the very severe weather. We were told to be formed up in our "jumping off" trenches to practise the attack at 10 a.m. It was freezing hard with a strong easterly wind which no clothes could keep out. " we had to wait until 12.30 before the brigadier arrived. That was on the 16th R, & the same thing happened next day; everyone was very peeved.

Luckily in manoeuvres all the details are worked out by C.O.'s, the brigadier just giving the different objectives & flank limits for battalions & barrage tables,

1st Battalion.

B { A { in two lines some 50 yds apart
Co. H.Q.          x
                100 yards.
D {          C {
    x            x

2nd Company of the front line of attack (here A & B companies), form up in the original front line trench – they are usually supposed to form up in special "jumping off" trenches, but there are never any, & only appear on the paper issued by the staff. At 3.00 A & B go out, just the first line, which gives as close a to the barrage as is healthy, that is until casualties from our own artillery become too numerous, & halt down, the second line to formed up below down 60 yds. behind, then Company H.Q. jolly out - flop down some 20 yards behind the second line. Just behind Co. H.Q. is the first line of Moppers up, who clean up the first trench taken. The second line of Moppers up, clean the second trench. They are taken from C & D companies, who pick them up as they pass the head of the good work is completed.

then the C.O. steps in. Stephenson was already working hard, for there is a mass of detail, & doubtless everything in, & we arrived solidly every evening from dust until 11 p.m. with intervals for dinner. Until you find out all possible happenings to be guarded against, you have no idea of the amount of instructions to be given.

I went over to see the 23rd N.F., my old Bn on the evening of the 17th, & heard about the raid; it had been a very expensive do — 8 Officers & 120 going over, & 2 or 60 coming back untouched. The idea was as opposite.

On the 19th we left for the south, marched through Béthune & Hazebrouck & anchored 1 mile beyond the latter. The Div! Comm! watched us march through Latters (I had never seen him before). I was at the rear of the Batt? leading my horse, & after passing I heard someone running, & shouts of "Brewin"; and found it was the Div! Comm!, one Nicholson, whom I then recognized as having been Station Staff Officer at Agra when I was a subaltern there. I knew him & his wife very well. They were charming people. He was very little altered, & we had a long yarn. This caused huge sensation in the Batt?, & endless chaff from Stephenson & Officers.

Next day through Aire to St. Hilaire some 14 miles. It rained solidly all the way, & the men fell out all over the place; the percentage short when we arrived at St. Hilaire was enormous, & the C.O. got it right in the neck from the brigadier; our batt? was last, but until in their Army H.Q.s. dreadful looking people. The billets were excellent at St Hilaire; we had the school Larue, & spent all night drying clothes. Next day via Pernes (Flanders) to Diéval, a plain march,

---

52

[diagram of trench line with labels M, A, N, C, O, B, K, D]

Bn! front line A, C, B, D. Companies made four points in between, to get into Bosch trench at the heads of the communication trenches, leading back from A, B, C, & A & D to form blocks shown !. These were to prevent Bosch pushing in from the flanks, & cutting our men off in the C.T.s. A was to have a party pushing down the front trench towards C, & B, D had parties pushing to their left towards C & B. C was to form a bridgehead at C, & from blocks at N, O to that no bombs could reach C. The main objective was K which looked, from aeroplane photos, like a Co H.Q.

A Co. ran up against heavy resistance (there is no doubt the Bosch knew of the projected raid) & M.G. fire from M, & only got as far as the parapet, exchanging bombs re. Daggett, comm'd ? A Co. was lost there; he was wounded & never found. B. Co never even got to the parapet (they had the worst Co (comm'd — ), & the men apparently never attempted anything. D met strong opposition, and had a bombing combat, but got in & reached towards B, but as B never came, they got pushed back & out. C got in & the party went straight for K, consisting of Lieut. Algie & 6 men. The support party to him had to go & assist the blocks at N, O, as the Bosch was messing in, & they had to keep the bridge had C for Algie to get back to Algie got to K. Ran up one dugout where they refused to emerge, & captured two prisoners in another, then dashed back again; all got back with two wounded. Daggett & A killed, Freeman ? D died of wounds, Heron Common ? C, Luton ? D, & Young ? A wounded, some 12 men missing & to do our aims were ridiculous. 1 D.S.O. Algie, & 4 M.C.s!!!

thick mist, roads hilly & full of corners, & surface (what front covering out) horrid. A great many men again fell out: they learned not to care a bit, & I knit the Officers were to blame for not creating competition between companies & platoons. Sibival was not fashioned & rationed – men's billets all over the place. We had the doctor's mansion (a princely place with a bath!). 2nd day we rested & cleaned up. On the 24th meandered to Chelers, just a morning march. The billets were bad, our temporary mess over the C.O.'s I slaying at the Curé's, a mad & disagreeable man, & a filthy house. We got our real mess next day (someone was awaiting burial there when we went in), & had comfortable sleeping rooms on the premises.

From this until March 8th, we practised the new attack over supposed copy of trenches (one could never have recognised them), & I guess it will be a go as you please & a scramble. It is best to have things all cut & dried, but one can see & hope for much to go according to programme.

Rawlinson (4th Army) came over with Allenby (our Army Comr., the 3rd), to see us practise. I was told off to go with "Rawly", he was a terror, perfectly mounted on a beautifully mannered horse, he could go any where & after watching the troops "go over the top", he galloped to the final objective to see them take that, some 2,000 yards & away to went full gallop straight over trenches & everything, just sailing away in a loose rein. What! I was struggling to keep my mare up, sometimes on her neck, then on her tail, down in trenches & ditches, a most unhappy journey, & how we got there without 17 tosses I don't know.

We had the first signs of spring on the 14th. 2nd Branch & needed them too, for it had been poisonously

the 101st Brigade were very sarcastic.

cold; unfortunately it was a bad false alarm; spring did not start until the end of April.

Haig came to see us one day. The bog-side was formed up facing the road, & H. came down & spoke to all Batt⁰ⁿ Comⁿᵈʳˢ. When we proposed marching past him on the road, but found we had all sunk in the mud, & it took some time to extricate ourselves — a very funny noise as we stepped off, squelching through heavy clay mud. He told Stephenson that our clogs were a very fine lot, as they were.

There was 3 inches more snow on March 5ᵗʰ, just below that spring was later! I got my first cold on March 7ᵗʰ. I'd had a most marvellously clean winter up to then, & after that never had another. As it was, I was quite fit again by the 9ᵗʰ, when we moved forward by bus.

We enjoyed the stay at Chelers though the weather was atrocious. Stephenson I had some nice rides round the country — it was a blackish clay though, very cold clay ground, & exposed to east winds, really worse to stand than the extreme cold of February.

We left at 8 a.m. & debussed at the junction of the Arras, St Pol, & Ecoivres roads at 11 a.m., & marched in to X Huts, a rest camp outside ACG, a most dismal place, all mud, & the roads cut up to glory. Luckily we were protected from the east winds by Mt St Eloi, on which stands the ruined church from which you get a first class view of Vimy Ridge. The latter was disappointing, as we expected a place like the Scarpe, & found a gentle hill, except at the north end which alone deserves the name of "ridge". It runs from just south of Lens right down to the edge of the Scarpe above Tampoux. We lived in hidden huts, which were not bad though dark, & had all tracks duck-boarded. We had 2 stiff-lines & mule lines

End Elevation. Just like a cylinder, cut in two, corrugated iron on wood frames, the corrugated iron all badly bent, lined with boarding. Wood floor, & stove, all huts are standardized, rather dark, the only light being through the windows at the far end. There at the door-end are in little bunks one on each side of the door, which Stephenson & I occupied, about 8 ft. by 6 ft. very cozy. There must be millions of them up & down.

every few days, as they soon were up to their tricks, and if they got down, never got up. The casualties in animals were terrific, & the men in rest had to bury them!

It was five miles N.W. of Arras, & we met the 102nd Brigade, the Tyneside Scottish, just off to the line, a brilliant with N.C.O.s. In the afternoon Stephenson, Bayliss (Acorn Adj'l) & myself walked up to Anzin to see A.Co. We was on detachment there. We made rather a bad break, as we read it on the map as about 4 miles, & it was close on six; and as we struck a blinding snowstorm on the way back, it was not a great success.
It cleared for the week-end, but all men were on working parties. Enormous quantities of stores & ammunition coming up, which had to be dumped, & every ounce late. I had the turned on including batman. I had captured a priceless batman, one J. Dleagie, a Scotsman & in private life, a traveller in tea. Christmas out there acts as one's escort, & so becomes more of personal friend, & I was lucky in getting J. Dleagie. The only thing was he used to worry me most infernally. He wouldn't let your mess off his sight. He & mad Lowe. Officers' mess cook, but was wearying himself to a shadow with worry, so Stephenson gave him to me. I found him attentive & invaluable.

Sunday, the 11th, was real spring like, sunshine, & able to sit without fires & with windows open, the stoves were not a great success, & the fuel very bad. The 12th was "freezer". Two of our aeroplanes came down near us, one quite close. The Germans approached much superior to us, & things were down with un- failing regularity. R.F.A. occupiers were wounded & wish as anything, & to make them more so they caught a telegraph wire on landing, & turned wild. They said they habit a dog; Lance, the Royal machine

---

343rd Division

| 101st Brigade | 102nd Rbde Tyneside Scottish | (Tyneside Irish) 103rd Bde |
|---|---|---|
| 15th Royal Scots | 20th N.F 1st Do | 24th N.Y 1st T.I. |
| 16th Do | 21st N.F 2nd Do | 25th N.Y 2nd T.I. |
| 10th Lincolns | 22nd N.F 3rd Do | 26th N.Y 3rd T.I. |
| 11th Suffolks | 23rd N.F 4th Do | 27th N.Y 4th T.I. |

being much superior, besides which they had no escort, & as they were slow-going photo & spotting machines, they made easy prey. On the 13th, the Bosch shelled our balloon with H.E. shrapnel & scared them down. You could see the observers sitting on the edge of the basket ready to jump, & you have to be very nippy, as you get mixed up with a mass of flames & ropes.

As I was bored to extinction, I went through a bombing course given by the Brigade Bombing Officer, a very nice sort of old gentleman, desperately frightened of Scotch Lad, killed on the 9th. The members were all throwing bombs. The course lasted until Friday, the day before we recommenced the line, & passed the time very nicely.

On Saturday 17th Mar, the C.O. Adj:, Asst: Adj: Signalling Officer, & myself went up to see the sector we were taking over. We rode to St. Catherine's on the outskirts of Arras. & from there walked some 2½ miles to the out line. Heavens! I had some grand walks up that way. It was a perfect day & we walked some mile up the Lille road, which was canvas protected on the east side, & was running along the top of the ridge. You could see the whole south of Vimy ridge, of course in Bosch hands, and they lorryed down on our line. The position was something like this. We then struck down the hill along a C.T. up the next rise & down a gentle slope to the front line. When we got to B, the Bosch started shelling A where we had turned off. He made excellent shooting, 2 S.7 every three minutes, all close round A; the first one hit someone on the road, & we could hear him shouting blue murder, & more so, after, the next two. Another man dashed along the road, & tipped him into the C.T. / jumping after him just as the next two came

(For sketch see over leaf. A.W.B.)

over; luckily they fell on the A side of the road. It was a very plucky action. Stirling (!?) (signalling officer) & Coat. the C.O. & C. & when he came to the top of the ridge. everything looked so peaceful, & the trench was so muddy, that we got out on top, but two minutes afterwards were very glad to jump in again, as we shower came over the M.G. fire. There was quite a big air fight on at a great height. We could count 16 aeroplanes, & could just hear the pop pop of their guns. Two machines came down in flames. The fight looked very pretty, the planes looking like silver moths in the sunshine.

We got to B.H.Q., a rabbit warren of a place with deep dug outs, & trenches up to 10 ft deep, just off the main C.T., & found Richardson commanding the 2/4 N.F. He was a XXth Hussar, & I remembered him at Lord. guard in the old days, so we had a great yarn. The front No Man's Land was all craters from mines blown, & says very disturbed looking, & difficult to find one's way about in, & we found that patrols were continually losing their way, & finding themselves walking into a Boche say, instead of their own line. The Boche line was hard to locate, everything was so smashed up, vastly different from Armentières. We wandered round the line, & out at 3.30, & so back to Ecoivres.

Sunday, Bayliss & I rode to Arras to see our billet if you spent one night in the town of Arras between leaving Ecoivres & taking over the front line, a very nice house in the Rue de Lille. The road back runs along the edge of the Scarpe, & the whole valley was stiff with guns of all shapes & sizes; the gunners took a delight in letting off their guns just as your horse was behind them. & the guns were not 10 yds off the road, so we had a cheery ride.

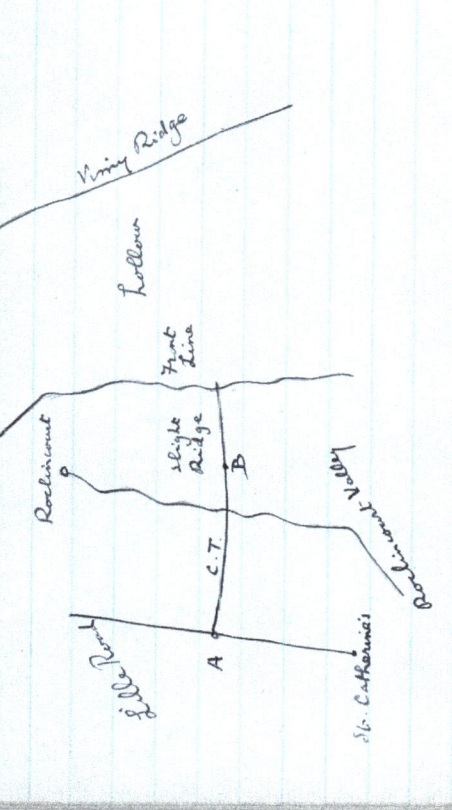

Lodja, a son of the Edinburgh professor, was a captain, an awfully good lad, some 6ft 5", & was popular in the line & envy to his height. He told me that he had given up trying to take cover, as the pain he suffered from so much stooping was far worse than being hit, so he used to 'stalk round out in full height, showing nearly to his waist above the parapet. I really believe that the Boche took him for a dummy — he gifted R. Academicians had sculpted & painted busts of men stuck on poles, & one used to carry them round the line to encourage the Boche to snipe at them. (They really were most natural), & as the Boche was pretty cunning he refused to be drawn. Anyway Lodja got a free and unexpected view of No Man's Land & the Boche lines, & was in great request by Stephenson on any question concerning them. The irony of fate was that he was killed in a dug out above Roclincourt, near Pérome by a direct hit from a shell on the dug out entrance. He was a very fine lad.

Monday we marched to Arras, it rained heavily. John Brewis called, & took me to dine; his Batt? was billeted Arras, very nice billet. Pads had great talk. At 2 p.m. on Tuesday we set off to the line. The men had gone in in the morning. He did not go up the Lille Rd. but up an endless C.T., coming from St. Nicholas, and then entered. The trench was fearsomely muddy, the only bottom to it being French mortar ammunition, petrol tins, & Amm? boxes dropped by foot-up Tommies carrying them up to the line. They received us with a very quiet enemy.

Next afternoon Baylies & I went back up the rise to watch the 11th (or 4th?) R.S. on our right do a day light raid at 3 p.m. There was some Ritz, & the gun couldn't start before 3.30, & as the raiders were all down in the sapa, & the Boche could see there was something up, they got a very unpleasant reception. We did too, for on the guns opening, he retaliated on our ridge, & we had a very lively few minutes looking for cover. He shelled us very heavily & well, only light stuff. Kemp, Hawk, goodness! & we found A.Co. H.Q. & dodged in there & couldn't turn out till until 6 p.m.; found Stephenson disconsolately surveying B.H.Q., which had also suffered considerably, all the wires broken, & trenches blown in. Kendrick (comm? 11th Suffolk) & Rose (comm? 15th Royal Scots) had been on their way up, & were very glad to fall into B.H.Q. deep dug out. Rose was so shaken though that he never came up again & went down before the Easter Monday.

Next morning we were awakened to very heavy shelling of the front line, all wires gone, & no communication with companies, so I went down with Baylies & found the two companies in the front line

I was sitting on an ammunition box in the sunshine reading the Daily Mail, & Baylies was using his glasses when he storm burst.

sitting very light but taking no harm, & breakfasted with them & so back. In the afternoon Stephenson & I climbed the ridge, & identified our programme for the 9th. It was really fixed for Easter Sunday but was postponed. 'Twas fairly easy to see our objectives, from the strips of trees which had been on the roadside, the railway, the Brown Blanche (a bag of bricks) & the Bois de Ca.B., which was just a cluster of tree stumps close to the railway. The only part we could not see was a dip towards the right of the attack which was reported as full of wire!

Next morning 23rd, the C.O. & I went to find a B.H.Q. for the show, found an old underground tunnel in a sap, & had a very fat time exploring it. 'Twas an A.1 place with two entrances, but no room for working; just a passage from the sap lead to the C.T. & we finally decided on a dugout 20 yds be-hind the front line, quite a roomy one.

On the 24th we went back to Arras, the mud was awful, went & saw John in the evening. Had a rotten job the next few mornings; there had been complaints of working parties being late, so the 2nds in Command had to turn out & parade these at St Nicholas at 7 a.m., Euston café, &c, & future parties parading until 10 a.m., so pretty peevish. Arras at that time n.t. much damaged, odd Zerox knocked, & cathedral & municipal buildings blown to ribands, but lots of traffic even by day light, though more & then the Bosch sent in big crowds of shells. At night it was one continuous stream of wagons, lorries, limbers, &c going at a fast pace all night long in both directions.

Ghastly snow showers on 27th, 28th, never shifted out of mess except for evening walk with C.O.

The 29th was very wet & we were relieved at 4.30p.m.

& rode back to Ecoivres, & missed a heavy shelling of Arras by Boché at 5 a.m. next morning.

Next day saw the 102nd Bde. & Col. Porch. He cursed talk of nothing else except the Push, rather boring, an awful pity he can't get away from shop. Stephenson never calls it except when we are working on details of show.

Saw two tanks for the first time. Kay promoted in three tanks per brigade (that is to 2 Batt:ns in first line). Well we never got further than Rocincourt, one fell into a crater in No Man's Land & the kind was afterwards found stuck, trying to ride over a Boché concrete M.G. post, all this long after the infantry had finished their battle, so that they didn't do us much good.

The horses were having a very different time, they of course lived at Ecoivres with the Quartermaster & those left out of the line.

It was the usual practice for the C.O. & 2nd in Command to take it in turns to go up with the Batt:ns, but Stephenson never stayed out, or missed a show, and I had great difficulty at first in persuading him to let me come up each time. His argument throughout, I found was quite sound, during my command. He was always wondering what the 2nd in Command was doing with the Batt:ns, & it was a miserable job, kicking one's heel behind at the Reserve Camp. Of course when there was a "show" on, the 2nd in Command, & proportion of company commanders, subalterns, W.O.s, N.C.O.s, & rank & file, had to stay behind, so as to leave some nucleus in case of a smash up. This term was learnt during July 16 when the whole Bde. stock & barrel of the batt:s went over, bar the Q.M.R., his staff, two officers a small working party, the result being that in some cases these officers were all that were left

by mere stick it O.K., rather ticked & peeved, but carried me well. The casualties in generals were terrific during March & April, & when we came out of the line after the Santa push, the roadsides were strewn with dead animals, & there were great piles also collected awaiting burial.

to carry on the good work. I found it a most difficult task both as Comp. Commander & Bttl. 2 Comm. & took the scales without him. He didn't "want" he was born Offr., NCOs & men in a scrap, nor did one want one's mantle to fall upon a useless lot, & there was always much searching of heart, & I had to revise myself all Comp. 2 Comm's kit to see they were playing fair. I remember one case at Passchendaele. In my own company was a lad of poor physique, low intellect, & still Coy Runr.; Pagan, the C.O., had the same ideas as I had, & personally revised kits with Comp. 2 Comm's. I had Cpt. Hes. sent out, & Pagan said "Why? All I could say was that he was useless in mud like one knew there would be, & that he'd be more nuisance than he was worth, but Pagan over-ruled me, & by a curious coincidence, he was killed. The faithful Gillespie, my Royal Scot batman, was the only man in the British Army who openly defied me. He refused to be left out, & though I used to pass the word to the Sergt. Major to order him to remain with the Rear party. He had to lodge off with the H.Q. & there me, & never missed a tour.

The 31st March & 1st April were miserably cold days with a nasty biassed wind, & even in Kervin-les Ypres was pretty poor in the daytime, really worse than in the line. He thought being outpost. On the 1st it looked really like snow, & did not disappoint us, as in the afternoon of the 2nd we had a blinding snowstorm, huge flakes & blowing horizontally, you couldn't see a yard. We had orders like it about the 12th April during the night. Stephenson & I were visiting the line (relieved for it was all very lonely, and one company was holding a trench running due east and west), at about midnight, when it came on, & for half an hour we were completely lost, struggling along, falling over wire, into shell holes & bombers, generally having a very thin time. Luckily the Boche was a long way off, and we were fortunate enough to fall in with a patrol of our own well out in no man's land, who said there was not the slightest danger of our being shot by the British, as our language precluded any mistake being made! & they knew who we were at once. Though Raphis, who in the absence of Officers had promised a company, said he couldn't understand both of us being out, & thought some other Sanbourny ruffian had found one!

We sat tight all day on the 2nd, and it got warmer after the storm, tho going though was appalling!

By time I made our 2 Lewis's [about ½ way to Arras], to inspect our next move, a nice chateau for H.Q. & staff, and Cats for the plavers, night shown on the edge of the Scarpe, rather swampy & nasty. Next day the Batt? was going to Louez, so I went up with Lewis to see the finishes from where we were taking over. I made to St Catherine's & then walked "Y". The mud was shocking in the trenches, & the Road shelled our C.T. right up & BHQ. Luckily generally just about 50 yards ahead of us. He apparently had been rather cross in our advance, as a CO of the C.T. from Arras, Sunday Avenue, was blown in. I had a whiskey & soda with Vignoles, 2nd in Com of his Coy. & chatted over things; he said their line had been pretty rotten for the men. The front line was nearly impassable from mud and naturally a lot of water too. Plenvicè & met, though the Boch laid a bullock the C.T.s pretty continuously. Of course he knew we were coming over, but returbur. I was pretty well done when I g.D. back to St Catherine's, but once I did get on top, we had a real gay splendy ride to Louez in record time. A Company Officers also/ived in the chateau with us & all officers ft together except gibbed H.Q., so I went & had a few rations of bridge after dinner, found everyone very gay & cheery.

Next day we didn't shift until 7 p.m. We had a warm peaceful day in the chateau. It was a rotten stormy night, snow & rain until we reached the ridge behind the front line, when the weather cleared, & the moon got out. Bayley the Adjt & I were walking together on top, when the Road opened out with machine guns, & we all fell. Eventually in to the mud, & to Batt. Q. where Gillespie was waiting with a knife to scrape me fairly clean. Batt Q. was like a rabbit warren with Lincolns & our men, landing & taking over, & the mess dugout was packed with two HQ., one couldn't get a lie down or anything, & as the All Clear didn't arrive until 4 a.m., we hadn't much peace.

On Friday the 6th, we shelled them pretty heavily, & they were busy cutting lanes through the wire with light guns. The place was littered with our spotting planes, & one got hit with swing them round, they seemed to last no time, & the number shot down was very large. Gunners were all over the place, L. industry making last dispositions & marking down last ideas, brigade bombers with working parties servicing down the trenches, making dumps of thousands of bombs & accessories, R.E's & more parties surveying & marking down things, dumping wire, pegs, &c., & in the night time a continuous stream of working parties bringing up T.M. ammunition, ordinary ammn., rations &c. till you couldn't get around, & the whole was like a sheep & cow fair, heard at a distance. I'm'd leave thought things never would do outside to themselves, & things like this were the main episodes of these last nights. Bayley & runner & going round, met a N.C.O., asked him how many in his party. "9" says he. "Right, tip them along." We flatten ourselves against the trench wall, & past come seventeen weary Tommies carrying Lewis Loads, barging into us, falling themselves, shouting "Here's No. 7 Party." "Pass the word along there", no one behind Pte Atkins. The endless stream goes on, & we get fed up with being banged into with every thud cornered thing under Heaven, so collar the last N.C.O. "Who are you?" — "24 N.F. No. 14 Party." (The word has apparently never been passed down by the party before to let us through) — "How many men?" — "I should have 10, Sir." — "Alright, pass the word down to halt the party after that." We count five down, & then start struggling down past the last five, find a blaspheming corporal wanting to know what ———— has stopped his ———— party", we mildly say "He wants to get through!", & push along past them. After going some 10 yards, meet another blaspheming N.C.O. who wants to know what the dash is; we try to push past him & get hopelessly jammed with two men bearing a rifle with some ———— slung on it. I tell Baylis to get up on top & give me a hand, & we slither up, take a line & move off. We start the Bosch with machine-guns, & we fall hurriedly back into the strong'g again, & so it went on all night. It took me the whole night to get round our sector.

Next morning, the 10.2 & 13th sent for the C.O. & so I went with him. He was sort of G.O.C. for the day, & sharing the Brigade H.Q. with the 10th, 4th, 13th, old Trevor Turner of Armentieres fame, an awful old woman. Ten Kenn was their Division said they wanted "Identification" which means "Prisoners" to find what they belonged to so as to check with "Intelligence". We rather looked down our noses, as we didn't want to get things by casualties. The day before the show,

"Intelligence" I might say were magnificent. They carried maps showing each Bosch Regiment's area & H.Q., & could tell you the numbers, "state of morale", whether vicious or harmless. That was easy though as all Prussians were vicious, Bavarians next till you got to the harmless & peace-loving Saxon.

however the dreaded Higher Authorities said "Let there", it was L.O. Trevor Vernon disgusted us greatly by hinting at having a pocketful of decorations for a successful raid, & Stephenson bluntly said his Batt" didn't want decorations in a raid, & he had knocked the 102nd into pleasant subalterns with N.C.O.s for unsuccessful raids) & still they did he want the inevitable casualties. Also what (at this time of the show) was the good of identification, as nothing could change the programme. Vernon quietly bluntly, & rather crossly, said he wasn't responsible for orders, & would we come carry out a raid at 10 p.m. that night, 60 men & 3 officers to go over, and prisoners to be brought back, no regrettable deaths by machine gun Amadytin to be reported. Stephenson put me in charge, as he said he was so fed up he was going down to Armagh for a good night's rest, as there wouldn't be much rest for him for some nights, so then he sailed off, & I took over.

I got three of the "Echelon B" officers for the raid. Cowan commanding C Company, Browne also of C. Company, & Stinton of A Company, & we had off'rs & N.C.O.s behind our right to spy out the land, we concluded the best place was just to the right of a mine crater, which would give the men some shelter, & if they saw it they would know more or less where they were, & so the moon would rise about then, they would have a fair chance of seeing it. It was going to be more on less of a raid. back again, officers to sound their whistles at the end of the time allotted & mark the men leave — anyone capturing more than one prisoner was to make the fact known by whistles, artist. meant "Clean Gone". It seemed a chancy do, but there was absolutely no hope of making better arrangements, seeing that the men had to be called for (volunteers), N.C.O.s & men picked, then formed into three parties. Cowan & Watson were to go over on the R.L. & Browne to go later with a reserve party. This would help for a forming up party in the Boche front line, further than which the reserve party were not to go, & also the same party could keep down the fire of any Boche in case they came up after the first parties had passed on. The idea was to lay odd sentries, as there were no time to clear dug outs, & Browne's party loaded themselves with bombs, to throw down any holes they saw. I then went back to TBHQ & warned them to meet me here at 5 p.m. with lots of men going.

Everything was fixed up, & it was a nice clear evening though chilsome. After tea, I went down & inspected the dug out for my H.Q. & Aid Post, with the doctor. He was a wild Canadian with a strong American accent, a stalwart who had won the M.C. on the Somme, & knew no fear. I hadn't seen much of him as Stephenson refused to have him in H.Q. & he said he had no way of carrying sufficient spittoons for the doc., & that without them. He was impossible; besides this he only shaved at odd intervals, & went to bed tight every night of his life when out of the line. He had the dug out about 50 yards back from the front line on own right, which was going to be BHR on the Push Day. It only had one entrance which of course was against it, but it was roomy, not too deep (in case it got the entrance blown in), & convenient to the front line. All the raiders were ordered to pass up the C.T. from the front line (running just the door of the dug out), on their return. We settled the arrangements. The doc. had the inner room, to set his stuff up in, & I had the outer one with runners, signallers in, & a small party to meet the Boche, in case he came over in the confusion at the end of the raid. We then went off, & I took the doc.

to dinner at B.H.Q., had a good tot of rum, & then driven again. This time right along the front line to our new C.D.
H.Q.

The line was in appalling state from all the traffic along it, the Boche shelling & the trenches were high god. Lovelessly stuck several times. The Boche had made several nasty breaks in the parapet, & it was exhausting work getting along & time getting short, for I wanted to get those with my crew before the raiders assembled. The Boche had shelled us some in the afternoon, but had wearied of it, & it was very quiet & still. I took up my post at the junction of the C.T. & front line, & presently the raiders appeared; Cowan & Watson soon got their men lined up along the front line, & there were no reported & compared watches for the last time. The moon was just beginning to show a faint light behind Vimy ridge, so the men had a good opportunity to fix the place of the crater, & also the comfort of knowing that there would be little difficulty in finding their way across & back, & as our guns had been systematically cutting the wire all division our front we didn't expect much difficulty from that.

The raid during the evening had been put forward to 9 p.m. & then back to 9.30, & no one was at all very certain as to when the barrage would come down. There was to be a 2 minute bombardment of the front-line after which it would lift to the second line well clear of the front and close support lines. It came on O.K. at 9.30, & away went Cowan, Watson & Co. Browne's troop was up a small sap, & joined the merry throng following on just behind them; they were all due back at the latest at 9.50 which didn't give much time for picking flowers or anything like that. I was watching them from the front line, the moon just rising & looking beautiful through the smoke & fire of the barrage, when I heard an oath from my elbow & Embry round saw the door. I was very annoyed as Stephenson had given orders he was not to leave the dug-out, but went there until I took him back to H.Q., for he was foolhardily plucky, & we certainly didn't want to lose him on the eve of the Push, seeing he knew all the arrangements, so I took him back to the dug-out about the Sergt. not allow him to leave it. The dve. was very peaceful. I went back to the front line, the Boche put up a few things hurried & lively aimed barrage on our front-line, & though things were flying about, it didn't interfere with the actions of the show. Ewin said got in with next to no casualties; a M.G. in a sap tried to be awkward, but Dr. Streit let from our barrage, & only he wounded two men.

It was trying work awaiting the whistle, however they came at last, & we saw the men scurrying home. The Boch was not long in popping up & greeting us with M.G.s, & most of our casualties occurred then. The men returned laughing & shouting, & saw two prisoners being shepherded in. one was sat on our parapet, & the language of his captors was most amusing; you'd think the poor devil had done it on purpose. I had a N.C.O. ticking off the men as they passed the dug-out, & went back to collect the prisoners' effects, before they were all collared. He was a miserable specimen some 20 years old, & very weedy & small. The men of course at once imagined they would all be like that, & it no doubt put them in better form than ever for the Show on Monday. The Doc. was very busy with the wounded; only one bad case, all the rest flesh wounds, & the men very cheery.

I could get no news of the officers, so went back again to the front line, where I had posted a guide, who said Browne had come back, & had gone out again to look of Walton & Cameron, so I toddled out too with a runner, & came across Browne very distressed. We watched & shouted, but could hear nothing, & his M.G.s were decidedly unpleasant. We were just coming in, when I again heard a very forcible oath close to, & found the dir. had got a bullet through his arm. I was very cross, but as his arm was broken, & he was in great pain, one couldn't say what one would have liked, so bound him up, & trotted him to his own aidpost. I cut the names to Bde H.Q., made a report out, checked the lists, & found 2 officers missing, 10 men missing (who turned up later) & 8 wounded, quite enough too, killed up the place & then slid off, as the relieving battalion was coming in.

I went up to our new B.H.Q., & found Kendrick there, having a feed of bully sardines & whiskey; he hailed me with delight, as he had heard I was missing (Zimmerman it was from Cowan). He was a Dublin Fusilier, having joined up in the ranks, & now commanded the 11th Suffolk — an awfully good chap. After I had fed, I pushed on with my runner, & got to Brigade H.Q. at midnight, & we rested there an hour when we were pretty done & had been in the morning. I saw also our Brigade H.Q. which had shifted up, an awful crush with the two staffs, & an awkward move went through, finally got away about 1.30. The 102nd & 103rd had done raids on their fronts, but had no prisoners taken (as the Huns wouldn't stay), nor many casualties, & were they never got there.

It was beautifully moonlight going down, & I was too weary to tramp through the mud, & my runner & I took a bee line over the top. The crest of the ridge was receiving attention (a military expression greatly used) by indirect machine gunfire, but more unpleasant than dangerous, & got in to 20.8 Rue de Lille (our H.Q. in Arras) at 2.45 & had a drink & to bed, no inclination or anything at all, my stiff Lord gave me an Ecros where Echelon B was for the Pack. So I wrapped my martial head cool-round me & slept (Yorkimite enough to have a mattress to sleep on) until 8.30.

Up to breakfast. Stephenson & all the scroungers came to breakfast. The former awful we wild when I told him about Gilman, the doctor. Then we settled down to a quiet experience. Everything was all cut & dried as it was only a matter of questions by Company Commanders on odd things, & a general talk by Stephenson. Whatever were at it, the playful Boche burst a shell right in the road outside our window; luckily all glass had already gone, but it blew in all the bardings & brought endless plaster down. When we had sorted ourselves Stephenson proposed an adjournment to a cellar in the garden, & he pushed off. I was bringing up the rear, as 2nd in Command should, when he burst a shell in the garden, & I was saved the trouble of walking down the few steps I still had to go, & landed in the middle of the cellar much to the amusement of the lads, after they had found I was'nt hurt.

About 11 a.m. we all dispersed, Roy to their Company H.S. for a sleep & I for Ennis somewhere a few miles behind Arras. I jumped a lorry, never asking where it was going, & found myself some five miles down the Doullens Road before I realized that it was not my right road, so alighted & walked across country to Ennis. It was a perfect morning, & as I only had my French coat to carry, it was lovely, bright sunshine & quite warm. I swore though I'd never wear Tommies' tunics again, they are much colder than ours. No lining, & short, & I suppered enough the night before.

I wandered into Ennis about 2 A.m. & found Lindy in command of B.C., just out from leave after being kit on the Somme & Cuy, a new Captain, 2nd in command D Coy & numerous strangers. We were all in one Nissen Hut,

---

20.8 Had a shell through it the very day after we left; it came in through the C.O.'s bedroom, & burst under the floor of the dining room, effectively finishing up the Lawot wrongly it on Easter Sunday.

& been latticed down. I was lucky in having a bedstead, a stand of timber covered with wire netting. We played Bridge most of the day, & I wandered round & saw the 23rd N.F.'s with Longhurst in charge, looking the picture of misery though not at missing the Show; had a marvel dinner, suppers, feed about 7 p.m. & then I was sorting out my things preparatory to bed, when a runner came in to say that Stevenson, the Capt. command 1 A.Co. had been hit, & would I go up to take over A.Co. I knew Stephenson had wanted to take me over with him to relieve the work after the Raid, but Brigade wouldn't have it, Lodge wasn't very fit, & Sherlock knew nothing of the line.

So, I packed up & got away my about 10 p.m. in my own time this time, managed to get a lorry as far as Morris. The road was like a skating rink with troops & transport, & we only went at a snail's pace. Gillespie of course came with me, & carried a wonderful array of "odds, stuffs." It was a wretched night, trying to rain & snow & much colder, the trenches & the line were packed with working parties feverishly trying to do in a week's work in one night & get safely out of the way before the Hayfall. So we went up over the top again. You're never seen such a mess as the C.T.'s were in, just packed with struggling with & Tommies towing up heavy loads of every imaginable thing. Our H.Q. had already shifted down to the raid dug-out, just off Padding tr. which was also the jumping off place for my company. I got in to report about 1.15 a.m., & Stephenson made me rest. I have some supper before going on. My Co. H.Q. was in a deep out about 80 yards away, towing him, told me to come back after I had taken over. I found Stevenson had been hit with a bit of shell through the shoulder ( they thought not badly, but he died about

10 days later).

The front line was like a fair, all sorts of men there, lost, strayed & fed up. Our men were mostly sitting on the parapet, as there weren't room for them all in shelters, or down a small sap which were handy. I got my subalterns & Co. H.Q. and cleaned the place & have a final to C4 (Off. Course I knew the arrangements as well as Roy did). Then I went round & saw each platoon, found every thing quite right, & so back to BHQ. The Board was shelling us freely, & I don't wonder when I heard the noise going on, men shouting & swearing & our working parties shouting for directions, & trucating to get their work done & away, & altogether the place seemed like a hive of bees. The infernal Boch had already blown in one Coll. House where we were preparing a final cup of tea for the men, & whilst I was at BHQ, a message came to say he had blown in the Rser, so the men had to went over without that comfort.

At 2.35, Co. Commanders finally compared watches with the C.O., & I joined my company & reported on the line to my subaltern. At 4 a.m. all sleepers were roused, & the Company took up its position along the front line, ready to go over. It was a miser-able mor-ning, cold & raining, & one felt an empty sort of feeling in one's tummie. At 5.5 a.m. the Batt" was all ready, & so that we only had half an hour or less to spare, one kept a pretty watchful eye on one's watch that last half hour, why I don't know, for there's no mistaking a barrage when it starts; and I suppose it is like waiting for a train, one always keeps looking at the time. It was cloudy & dark, much more even so than when the raid was on, & I thanked my stars that B. C. was the direction one, & that I only confirmed, through if B got off his line, I should have had to keep my right in touch with the 2 A Nut. (I had been down to the left company comm'g H.Q.T.R (the 6th KOSB.), leaving the right, I had arranged liaison duties with him. I had a stand the N.C.O. & 2 men to keep in touch, & as I proposed going with my Hd. Qrs. along the right limit of our attack. My little Hd. Qr. consisted of my C.S.M. & his batman, my batman, 2 stretcher bearers, who of course I should lose at once, 2 signallers, 4 runners & 3 general utility men, picked for their staunch character.) I selected me to attend on Gillespie, which meant that I should have an escort of five always with me.

At last it got to the final minute, the last few seconds & one got counting, and I believe they do at the starting & jumping races, 10, 9, 8 &c., & then up she came. I was pretty near where we had been in the raid, & so lived my own one.

They went as steady as rocks, swearing at the mud & wire but calling to one another to keep their dressing, just as they had at practice. The first wave, consisting of two lines (see opposite), pushed off & then l, my little party, ½ mt. Everyone was naturally most interested to get just as close under own barrage as he possibly could, & the front lines seemed, I can't admit any minute we would come on the Boch protective barrage in No Man's Land & our front line, & those who had got well over, would be cut off therein. I pushed along over most appalling mud & wire, & pulled up some 30 yards behind the 2nd line of the first wave, the first wave apparently having got as close to the stove as it could without getting scorched.

There was no long pause, & up went the barrage, the ancient fallacy of "charging & cheering" was blown to pieces, & we just strugged doggedly on pulling your foot from the mud & cursing at the delay. The barrage lifted to the second support trench, up & then Hun had only been desultory M.G. fire, it seemed like a desperate man sticking to it by sheer will-power, under very heavy & telling gun

---

First Line ———— A ———— 1 Platoon     } 1st wave
                B                    2  "       }
2nd Line  ———————————————————       
                         & Co. H.Q.

First Line  ———————————— 3  "        } 2nd wave
2nd Line  ———————————— 4  "        }

I had subridged a Lewis gun section from No 4 Platoon to come with Co. H.Q. or near them.

A most desperate & naked feeling to step up over the parapet into No Man's Land — a place when like the serpent, you had gone on your belly all the way up to now, & you felt as if your fabric a stitch of clothing on, & took the tip of a man I had met who told me he found a wonderful comfort in turning his collar up. It was such a different place to what one thought: one had only been in it with dark & now to be able to pick your way & avoid obstacles was quite exciting. The fireworks were gorgeous too, Shells bursting by hundreds, all explosives, with a purple orange glare, thick smoke, & up & though it all, the Boch periods "apparels for help in green & red & yellow stars, strings of pale yellow green lights — strings of ones lines the French used for them, & the knowledge that within a very short time down would come the Boch barrage & make No Man's Land a very unwelcomable spot.

The hoppers up were distributed as under.

```
                    No. 1 Platoon
                    No. 2  Do
           G.H.Q.   ⊗ Hoppers up D.C.
                    No. 3
                    No. 4
                    Hoppers up C.C.
```

D.C. Hoppers up dropped in the Boche front Line & — mopped up.
We went straight on, though the place was a shattered that it was impossible to jump the trench, & we scrambled in & out right & much.
C.C. Hoppers up dropped into the Boche Support Line.
The trenches were all given names for the occasion, like this

```
End of                British Line         End of
Batt'n                                      Batt'n
front >                                     front
          Boche front Line
          ─────────────────
             SLOM       SLOP
                Boche support line
                SUN
          SPUR
                    SOUR
```

Thus D.C. Hoppers up did their duty in TAN SLUM SLOP.

C ──────────────────── SPUR & SUN

We (A + B) went on & to R the Boche main Line SOUR.
C. Co. came on they picked their Hoppers up up & pushed on, dropping into SOUR to stay there whilst we took the main 1st Objective. D picked their's up from SLUM & & dropped into SPUR to stay till E A & B had taken the main objective.

---

would be to control his fire — it was wild & very sweeping, so that you really only got an odd bullet near you, as he was traversing the gun back & forward so swiftly — practically no rifle fire as I guess all the Boche were sheltering. Our 2nd Line, on looking back, seemed to be heavily barraged by the Boche, and also No man's Land, & C.S. support a bit beyond Heyed to the Boche front line. We had very few casualties so far. We found the Boche front line badly knocked up & hurried to get into & out of, not many dead about; a few prisoners came up from dug-outs, but as the "Hoppers up" were along with me, I had to pass on & leave them. It certainly gave one a crafty feeling, knowing that one had little chance of being shot from behind. There was naturally no shelling round us, though the weight of metal going overhead made a continuous swishing noise, & the Boche in SPUR were more stubborn than the front liners, & made it unpleasant with their M.G.'s & some as we passed over the remains of the front line, & pushed off to strike my flank party, a road which (as far as the Boche main front defences), was my right flank. The only signs of a road were the regular array of stumps of trees along, & I was delighted to see a party of British on the fair side of it, evidently 6th K.O.S.B.s.

We had made arrangements to meet with B. Co. but had to leave that to O.C. No. 1 Platoon, as I thought it more important to keep in with the KOSB's. The light was very poor, one could see about 100 yards, & some smoke shells from our guns blew back & sent waves of smoke back through us, & I was the more glad when I struck the road. By this time No. 1 & 2 Platoons had had become one Line, & 3 & 4 were closing up, so I sent a runner to push them back a bit, as I wanted a bit of extra push in reserve for our real objective, which was not due for some time.

One hadn't had much time to look around up to now, & very & after I struck the road & the 5th K.O.S.B.s, I couldn't go wrong, but

It was only 10 minutes from the start, & the light was still indifferent. The barrage was creeping forward & "Sour" river, so we pushed on, and before we got in were met by unaimed Boche shrapnel out on our side. Sour was really their first strong line, with the ruined Maison Blanche at it as a strong point, & was very relieved to see them hopping up out of the ruins; the men were awfully bucked too, as we had practically no casualties in my Company up to them, & we dropped into Sour full of man. It was far too wide to jump, & you scrambled down & up, & so scrambled over an awful debris of mud, broken timbers, barbed wire &c &c. The troops had been well trained & kept up to the creeping barrage beautifully, & one really couldn't do anything else; it was so wonderfully accurate, & each two minutes lifted 100 yards just like clockwork. I was pretty busy, & kept right up with the front line; we had to cross the road over to the right, & I had been greatly afraid that the men on the right would follow the line of least resis- tance, and edge down towards their left along the road. Mr. Fie, though, the Platoon Commander of No. 1 shepherded them across & planted his right hand section on the C.T. which led astray up to the Black Line, our objective (see opposite). Things looked very lonely behind for C & D was safely in their trenches, & there was only the wave (3rd Platoons) behind us in sight. It was turning up considerably in front though & there was considerable Boche's gun fire from the Black Line, & Lea & there you would see a man jump & sit down turridly, sometimes nursing an arm or a leg, or at other times just lying there. I was sorry to see our Lewis gun sections getting it rather badly - they were coming in too quickly for my liking. There's no mistaking a Lewis gun, & the Boche was cool enough to concentrate on them. I was told that one of them was apt to conspicuous, being some E.W.P. but even then I thought it advisable to get the gun men down in the C.T. which saved them off

it found poor Watson between the Boche front & close support line; he had been shot through the head, so could not have felt anything — he was the subaltern with the Saturday night patrol — & also two of our men killed.

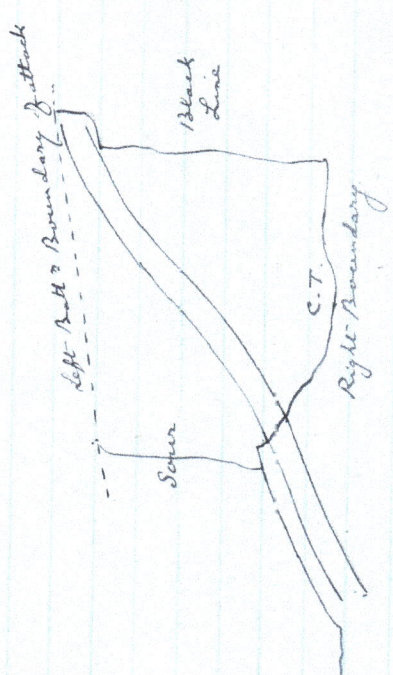

own direction, & I told Co. H.Q. was glad to lose his company. We had 20 minutes to get to the Black Line, so I had plenty of spare time to tidy things up a bit, as it was rather like travelling on the Met. Railway; one could have gone mushrooming; -com. fortably got back before you were wanted.

The K.O.S.B.'s lost direction a bit later, & were crossing my C.T., so I went & chased them back, as I had they got across. There would have been an unholy mix-up, & things were getting hotter & hotter; I wanted no extra work. People I have asked what one had to do to make one busy during an attack. Well, a company commander has probably 150 men under him, a good many of whom have a very vague idea of what their duties are throng[h] excitement; being under fire for perhaps the first time, & complete ignorance of how able to transfer their training behind the line to useful work over the top.

First of all you are responsible for direction, & being the right hand company of the division, made one more anxious about that than most things. You had to continually be finding out to your own satisfaction whether tow[n]el was being kept, & with the Rossville mess, up of our barrage it was quite difficult to keep straight; if one lost touch, one had at once to send out a patrol to find it again, all in the dim light of one Rx of an early dawn. This patrol had to be connected up by links (two men), who kept right of you or the patrol & if they lost sight of you, and then rain had to be sent out.

Then you had km lines, if two platoons each, these lines had to be kept apart — it is the natural thing for the second to hurry right on to the first from the start, and then you miss the object of being able to meet in the second line platoons mixt before the rush — because if they were all in one line, a good raking from a machine gun might flatten out the whole company: then you had to keep an eye on the second wave to see they didn't close on you. Then the men always bunch under fire for company's sake, & had to be scattered out to save them all getting flattened out. The noise was deafening as we were just under our own landing shells, & now just in front of the Boche landing barrage was pretty heavy on No Man's Land, & whenever a shell burst, there in the vicinity cleared off right & left to their nearest neighbours, & by the time they wanted the they were, instead of a line loosely spread out, bunches of 10 or 12 men all huddling together, & after each shell these bunches merged into the next & so on, till one good shell would have killed some 10 men & no good of say two or three.

Then your Lord & Hustle Lack men helping wounded & cooking !! prisoners. The wounded had all forgotten where the dressing station & aid post was, there was no trouble about the wounded; they wanted to be out of it right quick. Then I found we were approaching the Black Line (our objective); it was going up in smoke & flame, but they were doing some good work with the M.G.s. However I had to harden my heart & push up the two platoons to the leading platoons, I had just been along, seen all O.K. & got back to my H.Q. again when the barrage lifted & away we went. The poor Boche had stood the shelling wonderfully, but his M.G.s didn't like us so close & soon cleared out (not like they stood later on in the war, to the last), & we dealt in & had a few minutes lively mix up, men rushing from dug outs, & getting bayonetted right & quick (no time to ask questions), odd Boches desperately firing at one, & getting picked off, the mud, broken timber & wire mud & shell holes making the track like a Chinese puzzle. It was impossible to get down the trench, so I clambered out & went along it - a most heartening sight, our men full of good cheer calling "Anyone here", & if no answer, down went a couple of Mills bombs; generally the Boches came running up quick for the men were very excited then. Seems to a point where no men of mine were - I suppose a M.G. had caused casualties, & they had never clearly

I remember a case in point on 28th April : the 27th were supporting mine, the 24th, & after I had seen my men safely formed up & off, I was meandering back to H.Q. with 2 runners, when the 27th came along. By this time the Boche barrage was pretty heavy on No Man's Land, & whenever a shell burst, those in the vicinity cleared off right & left to their nearest neighbours, & by the time they wanted the they were, instead of a line loosely spread out, bunches of 10 or 12 men all huddling together, & after each shell these bunches merged into the next & so on, till one good shell would have killed some 10 men & no good of say two or three.

Burst shells
Own shells

Apparently the Black Line had only suffered in spots, for when I went over the ground in August 20, I found the part at Cam trench and to the right of it was as good as new, whereas to the left, on the 9th April it was badly knocked out. Of course all the limbering & support had gone, & it was now a sloppy trench like this [sketch] whereas at the time of the shove it was distinctly up [sketch] & down with big slopes to get in and out of them. All the slopes had slithered down making it much wider at the top, but still a magnificent deep trench, & when I saw the British line in '20 it was much more sloppy, & in the spring of '17 you had to crouch nearly all the way along the front line, & yet in 1920 the Boche trench was 9 ft deep still & an inch of course their front line was badly caved in through

what we had on the remains of ours. I was looking around, when suddenly I was pushed hurriedly I can only account for this "missing" of the bit of trench from behind, & had to jump into the trench, followed by a twenty on the right to some idiosyncrasy on the part of the gunners runner turning his & then jumping in. He said a Boch of Hartenstein; the slightest error in calculations would Officer had opened on us with an automatic, so we had to be sufficient, though unfortunately the ground in front of stalk him down. We had no bombs, & I good the Lewis (?), & behind the retreat Black Line had been straightened up, it was very sweat dodging round mounds & corners, & we couldn't see if there had been a concentration of never knowing where he was, or when he might shoot. We some place in front or behind. could see over many further down room, to know he must be quite close, when he suddenly gazed up from quite [Subsequently in conversation with an Officer he not- close. I had a go at him with my revolver & missed, think at Neuvrette, Royts discovered the real reason for & my runner got on, though to his arm. He tried again the condition of the trench. At the time of the German & so did I, & both missed, though his were very close. Offensive in the spring of 1918 it had been determined to us, & Ken the faithful Gillespie said he thought he to make use of this trench as a reserve line, and had got him; we dashed over & found him just thousands of men had been put on the work of digging gone. The faithful one had got him through the head. it out and putting it in order. The runner wasn't much hurt, & we bound him up.
A.W.B.]
The returned to go back), & Ken Hay stood guard over the dug outs whilst I went & chased them some men up with bombs to clean out the place.

My platoon commanders were jolly good, & I found them joining up their jumpoints, & sandbagging the Boch side of the trench to keep things ready for an early counter attack, after which I pushed out two guns well forward in shell-holes, to get a better hold over any attack. The platoon officers then fixed up their remaining sections in comfy places, & I went on to see the K.O.S.B.s I found them quite comfy too, & explained to the Company Commander my dispositions, & then back to see B. Company on my left; they also had got in very lightly & were full of cheeriness, & Wren then sent back the latter to 120 of telling of our doings. I had arranged for Wren to do all message work for Lock & us, as I was senior & responsible for the organization of the defence. The man Lawrence worked so well we were torn quite cooled down.

We were nothing to hine, & soon as we fell into the trench, the Black Line. The Official term for the line we had just taken was not very strong, & I think they had not anticipated such a good barrage, or anyway the weighty total of the place except for the dug-outs, was practically unrecognisable as a trench. B Company had lost two Lewis guns, which was a nuisance, on a complete loss, the gun + man, & unfortunately two more of the team Lewis had a direct hit, the other had a piece of shell through it, & the man carrying it. I Lundgb - all mine to for from spare,forms rather buckled, as they are vulnerable for defense by want a counter attack.

The Suffolks on our left were running about like rabbits, & assembled a lot of junts, their officers were not much good, & from what one could see everyone was souvenir hunting. It was a pity the Boord did'nt counter-attack then to straighten them up. Between us & the emplanting of the barrage, there wasn't a sign of anything doing, & evidently the man not had one to the "secondary buttery", or at any rate, true, a much much smaller proportion.

21 hours, I hand was now getting it good & lively, & the Reserve Batt. (13th Royal Scots behind us a Lieuths.), were hopping about like rabbits, dodging the shells, & they had pretty heavy casualties coming across.

Time passed quick enough, & at 7.30 a.m. we formed up under the barrage. It sunken road was our immediate objective, & we could only tell it by old tree stumps seen dimly. However, I had my CAM hands as a guide, & couldn't go wrong. It was quite light now & the Boach apparently very annoyed by the moment of a stoll. Crystol staff too. He was putting over, we were quite unmolested, as we formed up, & away we went again at 7.36. It was drizzly, & the mud was very sticky, we moved down a slight slope towards the sunken & second about. The wire which was supposed to be very thick beyond the sunken road, too soon as the barrage went beyond the sunken road we got considerable rifle & machine gun fire, & men began to go down fast. I slipped on the Lewis gun into CAM, landing me with two above ground, & Lieut a small party of bombers in front of them to clear out CAM as they went, but there was none in it. Everyone was laying against the skinners of the barrage, 50 to each 2 minutes, & the language against the gunners was choice. However the men during the waits got into shell holes of which there were any number, & where out a bit ability at going on when the barrage lifted. I had to move 3 & 4 platoons back as they were too close in 1 & 2, getting their & share of casualties, & gave each section commander a free hand to handle his own section, regardless of the wave as a whole. I was pretty fed up when I got back to CAM (it was very exhausting in the mud), so pushed right on with the bombers, & had a bit of a rest until the re-mainder came up again. We were jolly glad when the barrage lifted off the sunken road, & we pushed in, & fell into it, 3 & 4 jamming gladly in the rain in spite of the rain. The Boche stood up to receive us with open arms, & I am afraid some of them got it in the neck, for it was too much to expect the men to receive them as brothers after having been so shot up by them. So far I hadn't an officer killed or wounded, & found B had only had one wounded. Our men though had copped it pretty heavily, mostly wounded of course, & B. Co. had lost nearly a whole Lewis gun section (& gun of course), & through running into a burst of M.G. fire. This left them with only one gun.

We didn't stay long in the sunken road, Capt I & 2 then & up (there were two big dug outs), & 3 & 4 pushed right on into VOSS & JOY trenches, the men from here had removed to the cutting. The wire was not to serious as expected, & was well broken up, but the M.G. fire from our left was heavy, & made one think of stormy times when the barrage left the cutting; at present it was cutting chaps out of the chalk cutting, & having a real good time.

C. & D. Coys came through us, & formed up under the barrage pretty well together. "A" also went off the Blue Line, & C. & D. went on more or less together. They had half Lad pretty heavy casualties, mostly in No Man's Land & the front line, & they & we ran in to a real Lefty M.G. fire, which came from the remains of the wood, & was very difficult to locate. It was too warm, & everyone lay doggo for awhile to consider the matter. C & D had automatically (without intention) side-slipped to the right, which left the ground opposite the wood bare of men, & the M.G.s not having any worry from in front were calmly enfilading C. D. and keeping them down with a vengeance. I ran along JOG to the rear, but he had slid forward & talk to Martin, commanding D, so I walked in toward Flatt & Thorburn, the two other officers of B, & told them what was happening, & suggested opening with their Lewis gun through the range was pointblank, & would send up one of mine to give them a hand; I could hard & sent up a L.G. & found my men losing up in C. & D., so lying through shell holes r... it was impossible to stop them, or perhaps just as well, as we had a Bath? behind us, & C. & D. getting thin wouldn't stand a lit of thickening. It was very unpleasant going up, like an aerosol, just alive, & one jumped, Dodged and ducked any number & batsman always Rarity. C.H.Q. I had completely lost, though no doubt they knew where I was. Just as I got up to the sunken front line of C. & D., I saw a very brave thing. Flatt had got the

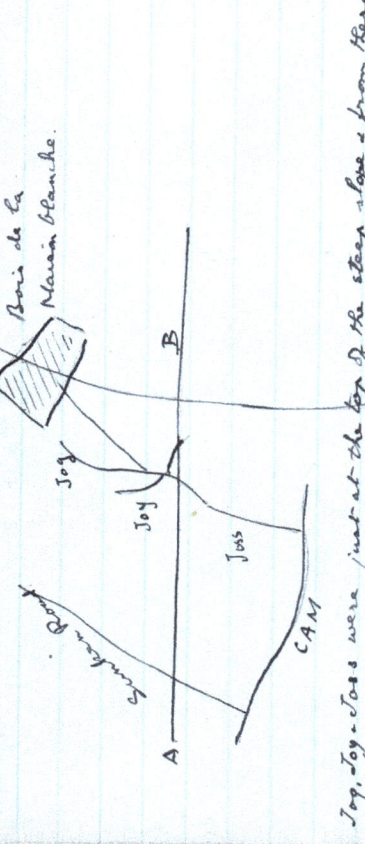

Joy. Joy. Joss were just at the top of the steep slope & from here it was a gentle slope up to the cutting. Section through AB would look like this:—

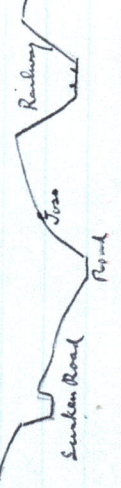

"The wood" rather puzzled the C.O. in his Operations Orders had warned C. & D. to be ready for "wood fighting" in the Bois de la B.B. well since these Orders were written, the wood had not escaped shelling & hadn't a single trunk more than two or three feet high. The undergrowth & tree tops of course made excellent cover, but the wood was much too small to even have a dog's chance of a wood-fight!

113

Lewis gun fairly plainly the same wept in, & the M.G.s were a bit upset; one stopped worrying us & made to turn on the L.G., when Platt jumped up & waving his men on, dashed at it. He was shot nearly at once, a young Thurburn jumped up & dashed off; he had a Lager dog & no doubt saved our way over. The M.G.s were worried over his new attack, & momentarily the fire died down, & we up & off, the whole lot together, C. & D. & myself & runners, & my own company, racing (a good wad through the mud!), to catch up the rest & to get out of the inclement weather. We met a good deal of rifle fire, but my Lewis guns had been plastering the cutting top, & so had kept the Bosch down to the last moment, & we hadn't far to go before we were too close for Mr. Bosch, & he disappeared as we went.

To go on about Thurburn. I heard afterwards that he was shot through the shoulder. Did didn't stop the lad, & he ran on & exchanged revolver shots with the M.G., but unfortunately was killed.

The mix-up when I got to the top of the cutting was great. Bosch running about like rabbits up & down the line, & over the tank, no opposition at all, & our men had some lovely rabbit-shooting, than up I hunted my Lewis gun, & the old Bosch gilt real lively. Some running for the barrage some 300 away, & trying to run back again, where they found that so unhealthy, at close quarters & lunge through throwing themselves in shell-holes & anything to escape the fire. Rose in the cutting had all disappeared down the dug outs, so we went down and put bombers up on the job, & they just the sand up out of the shelters. They must have been packed.

I picked up the Lewis guns & having been to rear of coy & the companies & remnants, went out and posted them well forward to deal with counter attacks. Then I went along & found the Suffolks on our left. They had only got in after we had set the example, & had also been badly handled. The cutting on our right curved, & then petered out, so I put a Lewis gun to cover the end, (not a road there), & went to look for the K.O.S.B.'s. The cutting ended in a level crossing, & then ran into another cutting, like opposite, & I saw a very pretty scrapping on the next cutting. The Boche was fighting quite well, & so were our men, one lot was working up to the level crossing (R), & there was any amount of uproar. They were plastering the cutting with Lewis guns from a slope behind the valley, & finally I heard a volume of fire that they were enabled to deliver. The cutting Boch came running out of it at "K", & ran into my Lewis gun, & there were some quite lively scenes in the cutting. I wandered back, until things had quieted down, & found they had discovered Trevan, the O.C. Road on the Saturday in a dug out with a bullet through his thigh, but sleeping very soundly.

Trevan had wanted out men room, & towed all of us, & even Tynesiders, out of our section of the cutting, & then gay Carlo were on the [?], & chalking the names of their Batts on the dug-out entrances, & no one got pas mad with them & chased them.

He could only gather about 70 men in the cutting for company work, & Trevan handed them to me, & got them on digging posts along in front of the cutting (100 yards).

Trevan's message to BHQ got there at 8.30, giving success at Blue Line.

Casualties 2 Officers killed (Hewitt, Thurburn).
6 " " wounded, 2A, 1B, 2D, 1C
3/0 other ranks, killed wounded a missing

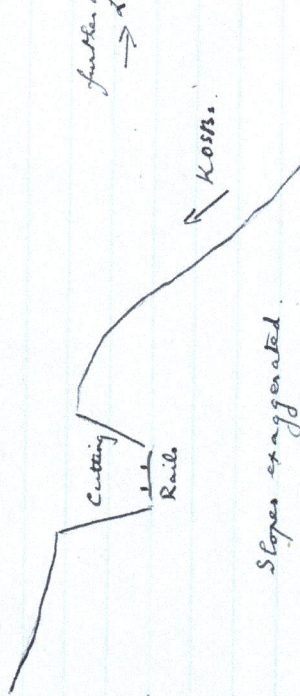

Slopes exaggerated.

I had a Johnny wandered down, a Company Commander too, from the Suffolks who asked "How do you defend a Railway Cutting?" - he was quite at sea.

2/0 much Café!

9.30. B ₹ H.Q. moved up & dug out in Black Line, e.g.
very considerably shelled up to 3.20 p.m. when it died away.
12.16. 15 Royal Scots passed through us to take Brown &
Green lines, about 1500 yards away each; looked rather
a forlorn hope as 15th were under 200 strong; but the
Boche luckily didn't known, & had nearly given things
up. We had a very anxious time in the Blue Line. I went
to see the 'Boris'. I found the Boche machine gunners all
laid out by their guns, poor Thunbeam only 20 yards from
them. Prisoners streaming away westward, only too glad to
go. Sometimes shepherded by a wounded Tommie, but
mostly all on their own, & running like Billy-oh! - a
fine lot of men generally, though some awful weeds
amongst them. The weather brightened up about noon,
and the sun actually shone for awhile, & we dried in it.
Jaunty ragamuffin looking lot, all torn with wire and
plastered from head to foot with mud. Felt awful
hungry for the first time, so had a snack & a good
pull of rum, & felt much better & fit to tackle & something
proper.

The shelling was poor, from a Boche gunner's point of
view. I suppose the situation was too obscure, & we were
too far forward. Round the Boche front Line & Black
Line there was considerable activity, & we rather suspected
at the thoughts of BHQ threading their way across, with
no 'attack' to hearten them, & I can guess from knowing
Stephenson, that the language would be lurid! HQ. in
Learoid Cabin, had got as far as the sunken road, only
sunken on one side, & had taken shelter from the rain
there pending a lull in the storm; shortsighted on their
part, for it was all sunshine & comfy where we were.

H.Q. were greatly bucked when they did arrive though
the Rank & File considered them & pull long faces, but

Staggers from the left, who had joined the battalion on the left, came up, and also many very slightly wounded, who had sat down to get dressed, & had found themselves not seriously damaged, also some stragglers up who had stayed to make certain no one was shot in the back, so that really we were progressing.

I pulled the 15th R.S. for they had a long walk to do.

"If they did meet serious resistance would have a thin line, & we congratulated ourselves on having one over Fritz. It was the difference between two men with appointments at the dentist at 10 & 11, & the 11 o'clock man having to sit in the rest room, & hear the groans of the victim knowing his turn must come sooner or later. Worse of the 15th, had gone sick, & Lodge, a brother of Prime Lord Real to take over only a day or so before, which was rather bad luck on him. They disappeared over the ridge some 500 yards away without any trouble, & as there was room no danger of counter-attack without warning, we set to sort things & rest out.

The C.O. decided to make two companies of it, so took me as a guide at H.Q. and I with Cavenaual, Warren to talk C & B, & Martin, C & D; we signed up the Lewis guns & found six had gone west. We had together a good night, at any rate free from the worries of a news unknown front line, so went gaily up to the Brown Line about 6 p.m. & got comfily in a very good trench. However we later got orders to go up on to the left of the Lincolns. the 15th R.S. & the Lincolns were so decimated that they couldn't hold the length of front, & the Tyneside on our left hadn't arrived, so we journeyed up front along a bit of the Green Line, & refused our left along Torey trench — no signs of the Tynesiders beyond the Blue Line, & no one knew where they were — just like them!

Master G. H. Osgood

Tuesday 10th April

H.Q. remained in the Brown Line, a small dug-out, fairly crowded out; however as the C.O. on myself was provisionally around most of the night it didn't matter much, & there was plenty of time for real sleep later. Rations came up O.K. about 11 p.m., no food contained as in future days, just cold meat & bread, some rum, which was very welcome. I slept like a top between times, & felt quite fresh at dawn when we all stood to, to see if the Boche was going to try & get his own back, but he had had enough, & did n't even shell us.

Spent the morning in tidying up our line, which was complicated, as we were facing kind of mostly across the place where the Tynesiders should have been, however we met with no distractions, & at 11 a.m. Gavin & a patrol went out & found a battery of 3 5.9 from which the Boche cleared on sight. Plenurie at a sign of Boche for 100x East of us. What a pity, if only we had had a few more divisions, and our guns could have come forward, we could have gone miles. The guns we heard, were all bogged coming up, & of course when & ever got fairly in, it stopped the whole lot. I do n't wonder for the ground was bad enough for a man on his feet, & what it must have been like for gun teams & caterpillars I don't know. Anyway they couldn't come up, there were no reserves of troops, so we had to sit tight & watch the Boche, in full view, calmly digging himself in some 1500 to 2000 yards away, & not a shot could be fired at him. It was galling.

In the afternoon they shelled us freely, & we were sorry to get the men into some strongpoints the R.E. had had dug near the Brown Line. The Tyneriders arrived in the evening, & so we handed over our piece of line to them. They were very angry, looking on themselves as en- titled to a rest, but we denied out that we had done

one night's duty for them, when we ought to have been resting, & weren't going to do any more. There was some snow in the evening which didn't make things any more pleasant.

The night was mild, & I was jolly glad we were not in the front line. Romy L as it was, it was horrid. Stephenson & I went round the Strong Points at midnight, just to cheer them up, for the men were beginning to feel the strain, & we had all been wet through & chilled to the bone since Sunday night; I found two or three of the officers pretty near played out, & to send down to Erme (?) for others to replace them. They had had a very heavy time for it in the shelling. B.M.C.Os they were practically sharing 24 hours work in 24 hours. Most of them though I were in good form, stalwarts like Martin & D. Warre & B, & them being very fit. They were too were anxious for the men, who they said were getting very tired, & their feet were giving a lot of trouble, standing continuously in slushy mud would knock most men's feet out. Mine I had rarely felt, & certainly they had never been warm since Monday morning. Stephenson wrote out a stiff letter to Brigade, saying that the men were & rarely at the end of their tether, & that he wouldn't be responsible for them unless they could roll out a definite limit before relief was due. We got completely lost going back to H.Q. The snow was blowing horizontally, & the wind had screwed round & it was than off again, & for some time things to us had got lost again, but ran into the ration party near our shelter, & so got in, done to a turn.

Wednesday we moved again, handing over the strong points, A & B, to the front line or Capt of Lincolns, C & Halsey

Wednesday 11th April

Wednesday 10th April

On the morning of the show, Bay Riv had occasion to take a message across to the 102nd Brigade H.Q. (who were with the 101st) & reported dozens of rifles & bayonets stood up outside the dug outs behind the Jumping Off Line, & we heard later that the 102nd had had great difficulty in getting their supports over no man's land, & that in fact ½ of men had gone till dusk on Monday when the shelling died out. Rotten! Their brigadier was sent home, & also the brigadier of the 103rd who totally failed to make any impression on the Bond Line on the 9th; luckily for them, when Hay attacked on the 10th, the Bond had cleared! — pretty rotten too! Bob Herm— commanding the 24th (1st Grenade Btn.) was killed in no man's land trying to get his men on!

Wednesday 11th April

in support. At noon, the Tyneriders rom left Bay stood their ground (from us to the left, the Brig had beat back badly, & they managed to come level). Luckily Hay had a soft job, just a few machine guns, with not much fight in them. We had a good view, as we were on higher ground. The H.R. Bri— on our right also pushed forward, & joined up with our front-line, so that we were relieved of flanking defences which saved lot. At 7.30, Bay Lies (Lincs. Reg?.) & S. Her ranks recon— noitred a dist. some 800 × 1000 × east of our line. This had been occupied previously, but now the Bosch had made the Gyppy Gavrelle Road — temporary line stop-shops. (Bay crews held the dug outs made before.) & had withdrawn on it. At 6.30, C & D moved up into it, & the H.R. Bri— conformed. The Tyneriders learned that Gyppy where they were, so in a short-time we again had a defensive flank to make. Cpt. 7.13. A & B went up to support C & D, owing to our left flank being in the air, so then we were again with the whole Batt? in the front-line.
It rained heavily all afternoon & evening, & when Stephenson went round at 11 p.m. he came back very perturbed over the state of the men. They were damp in & very exhausted. The med. & strain had fairly knocked them out. I went round about 3 a.m. Luckily a C.T. ran from the gun pits where 13? H.Q. had been made to the front line. I was shielded at the men, & the officers said they had the greatest difficulty to keep the men awake, & joined me, wouldn't this if ex laudatum. Hay, the officers, were wonderfully cheery. & I had a water bottle of rum with me, I was very popular.

Stephenson was so upset over the men he told me direct to drill H.Q. with a free hand to say what what.) felt, & also a letter for the S.O.! — Brigade had sent us a message that Bri? could make no promises as to relief. It was a relief to get a real walk, & be able to pick your way, & get on the Arras Gavrelle road at the ridge top & had a very nice walk to Arras. Though the ridge was appalling.

Thursday 12th April

Guns stuck at every point, & in trying to get them out, they had made a regular bog all round them. You're never been such a sight, & so many guns Hors-de-combat. JB rode home about 10 a.m. I was a wretch, torn to shreds, & mud from head to foot, not a wash since Sunday afternoon. Saw Brain, & S.O.1. & gave him Stephenson's letter. Oh he said, your men have done splendidly, & D.C. Stephenson to, & they are alright now, as there are no more operations for your brigade! I said it wasn't operations, but pure exhaustion that was knocking us out, & that we could stay on. Brain poo-poohed it, so I got wild & told him I hadn't seen a brigade or Div'l Staff officer beyond the Blue Line (The railway cutting), & that they knew nothing about it. He got quite huffy, & wanted to tell me he knew all about its things, & of shortly contradicted him, & told him I would pilot him out — to safer himself, as he wouldn't believe either Stephenson or myself. Lichtchen, the Div'l general apparently had heard some of our trouble & came in to was very amused at my appearance, & didn't wonder; was awfully genial & made me stay to an early lunch, & then said Brain should go & see to it, one, Brain which I seem at all optimistic. Lichtchen was charming, & wanted to know what I was doing up there, & all about things. Then Brain & I sat & wrote on horseback, rode to the Pont de Jour, & then I took him down to Stephenson. He was not to cockahorse when he had got there, but Stephenson insisted on tiggering to the line, & just as they got to the french two poor lads died of it in front of them. This frightened Bn. Brain up at once, & he said. — "That's quite enough for me, you must be relieved," & set off back. The men perked up when we could give them some hope of relief, & were dog-tired & worn-out; the rations were of course still cold, but — we got quite a bit of rum into them at 5 p.m. the troops on our right attacked again, & the

Thursday 12th April

Road shelled us unmercifully luckily not for very long. At 8.20. we were relieved by a Batt? made up of Lincolns, 15th R.S., & went back to our Strong Posts near the Brown line. Tpy stalled us Lewis guns at 9 p.m. Had a nice hotday.

Friday, April 13th, we were ordered back to the Blue & Black Lines & after dinner to the Rclincourt Valley. We went back as far as the crest of the Vimy Ridge for continuation thereof which end, just above Farnpoux & the Scarpe J. in a C.T., a fearful back-breaking walk, mud well up to the knees, & real sticky chalk mud at that, we were the last to go, as we had to wait until the incoming Batt? had taken over all our line, & we had received the magic words from each company "Relief complete". It was all very & rather a strain later on, on relief nights, awaiting that message. The Bosch was very knowledgable as to relief, & we never knew if he would come over my lot in the pandemonium of "Raff in Raff out." with all C.T.s chock-a-block, & everyone thinking much more of relief than the Bosch. I remember I relieved Richardson of the 26th N.F. just south B Gavrelle on my 2I.C, & the last message come through from my last company to say "Relief Complete" "well", said Richardson, "Thank God, I'm out safe." I'm "always on tenterhooks till I got my men out of the front "line." Just then outside the B.H.Q. a big dugout in the Oppy line, a 5.9 burst with a thundering roar. We all ran up & found 16 of Richardson's from Cadis laid out flat. Stephenson & I stepped out onto the top, & walked down the hill towards the railway. It was pitch dark so saw own chaps: lots of them could only just hobble, — some were being carried down on a fel?'s back: their feet were in a dreadful state. We had lunch at the railway & then over the Black Line & down to Rclincourt Valley, where we were apportioned a very draughty dugout: not a downstairs one, but one dug into the side of the hill with two entrances; still it was peaceful. There we met Sharrock & the details from back. Sharrock had whiskey & soda for us & we pledged the 16th R.S. in a Royal Drink. Then I went round A & B to see how they were, & Stephenson Co. D. he was very doubtful as to how the men would ever get out, as we had still a good mile or two to get to Bras, but they were very cheery. & Sharrock had big dixies of hot soup, & he lived with us, & in a very short time, they were much as before the show.

We slept there that night, & next day had kitbed & cleaned up, shaved & generally became respectable again. Since last of the men had cut the skirts off their great coats — not good for the coats, but quite excusable, seeing that the tails got too heavy with mud that no man could carry them. There was an awful shortage of equipment, Lewis gun ammunition drums were missing by hundreds. It was a very [wet?] day & after lunch I went over & did the attack on my own. They had tidied up wonderfully. Legion of Johnnys all over the place, & all our dead from the early phases were laid outside a big crater, in which they temporarily buried the whole C.R. after a staggering C.P. to see, when they were all collated, but as it was the damage of a whole brigade & nearly another, I suppose it was not excessive. They had buried the killed at the railway, just short of the Bois de la Maison Blanche, from which came most of their deaths. That & Thélus were buried there too, but returned afterwards, outside Arras. I saw the two tanks which were topped. Morval & beginning to do somedaw; one was struck, by my [to climb] a Boche machine gun post in the front line, & the other never got over our front line. The tank game up the ghosts in Roclincourt valley & never ap- peared on the scene. There were some damned civilians looting dead Boches & others & ends, so I scared them with a couple of shots from my revolver, & they ran like hares. It was sickening to see them, some of the Bosch were pretty well stripped.

We rendezvoused on the Lille Road at 9.20, & marched to Arras. Luckily they had provided a couple of lorries at our urgent request, for the worst cases, & we met again outside the Cirès, on the St Pol road. There we had soup & rum, and tea & rum, & luckily it was a fine night. They slept, and about 1 a.m. we entrained & away went, finally reaching a village called Aver- doingt, some seven miles from St Pol, at some unearthly hour: anyway I know when I finally reached my billet, after seeing everyone safely in, it was just breaking day, and a bed with plenty of clothes on — I was too dirty to beat the sheets — slept like a top & was awakened for lunch at 2 p.m. After lunch moved billets which were quite good, & back to tea at 5:45, & then a carol ball by a warm fire, of the sumptuousness of it, and sitting after it in pyjamas right against the fire with a mpt was a thing not to be forgotten. The C.O. & I had two teeny bedrooms leading off the mess room, which also was hopefully warm. Not late to bed for we still had many arrears of sleep to make up, & didn't we sleep too.

Next day was given to the men to clean up before starting refitting, so the C.O. & I just went round & saw them all, & then left them to themselves. They were all very cheery & mending fast: some feet of course had gone too far, & had to be evacuated, but they all begged not to be sent away. Our M.C., a nice lad, had had rather a fierce time. He had come up on the Sunday night before the show to replace our doc., wounded the night of the 7th., & had never been in a shower before, but had done very well. Though naturally he was dog tired

It snowed most of the afternoon, so we sat round the fire & got up to date with the news.

Tuesday 17th, horrid sleety day spent in reorganizing; getting the men clothes & equipment. A new draft of 170 arrived, & it was funny to see our unshorn shrunken men, though most of them had been wounded before. We had a good percentage though of ex-cavalry men, as they were just beginning to take the men training at home as cavalry, to fill up the gaping holes in the infantry, & excellent men they were too. Our draft was mixed, I mean from all corners of Great Britain, evidently the beginning of the order not to have all the casualties from one area, when a batt'n got wiped out. Yet in the Somme some areas were completely wiped out, & naturally it was very hard on a particular spot, so from now on they mixed them well, so that casualties were scattered over all parts — a very sound idea, but not a Territorial in our a.K. trelve at all.

On the 18th we inspected the new draft; a very likely lot, mostly veterans, whilst I remember the cavalry turned out A/I Battery. "Eclat", as Jack Wray said, very keen, very smart, they, in never unimpaired tho' then old jetblack, through goodness knows how, for an early knock. The troops were charged with looking by the Army Corps a Division: we had a surprise kit inspection & captured 1 German Testament! Jammie very sorry some ties of carting round soaprun & though they certainly packed anything useful & interesting from the Bosch in the Blue Line, the next few days fed them up with carrying extras.

Evans, Bayliss & I in the afternoon went & inspected the Trench Mortar school in the next village, which contained every describable native of Bosch in the ways of bombs, English & Bosch, — from the Flying Pig & Cylinder some 2ft 6 high & 2 inches diameter, down to the Oyster Bomb about as big as the palm of one's hand, with legs sticking out which detonated the bomb on hitting the ground.

Oyster bomb

137

The egg-bomb (Body) was a beauty, just about the size of a hen's egg. "you could throw it 60 or 70 yards - more moral effect than personal damage. The pine-apple, a rifle grenade, about 5" inches long x 2½ across, all corrugated, and which "on personal experience was very effective. Next day the Bde Commander (Rickham) came round to see us, so we had Batt Parade on the road, marched past him then formed up in a mob to receive his appreciation; he was very nice & most complimentary.

Next day more tidying up with a shift entailed in view; on Saturday the 21st we sallied off for the skies again, no blooming lorries this time. Rough as it was a charming sunny spring day we didn't mind. We turned off at lunch time into a wood & fed: violets & anemones were beautiful, & a real spring-like about things, nice & warm sitting around. Then on by rain & reached Hauté - Avesnes about 4.30, very good billets - poor mess. The village was on top of a Ropt hill above the main Arras St Pol road about 2 miles short of Etrun (The rest camp I went to on Easter Sunday); next day went on to Etrun to our old R.Q. very cold & cheerless, a good frost at night, hot morning. The Butt set off for Arras en route for Fampoux, & I, & my Echelon B readieward to a place called Tennant-Seville a village on the Scarpe, entrenched by shot & shell, & looking very nice & Lamelita in the sunshine. We left at 6.40 a.m. & desperately cold it was, but the sun soon warmed us up, & we had a very comfy walk. I found on my arrival that I was Brigade Bidding Officer, but that there was no Town Major or Official of any description, to not down & layed in the sun. The stuff walked arrived about 11.30; Buck, 2nd in Command of the 11/8 Suffolks was a very objectionable & tried to boss the test, but the Staff 2nd ignored him, & visited him a lot of what he was going to have. Token Turk had gone & said:- "I always take up that suit for the most objectionable unit, then fit the rest out". I Drowlis's got a topping mess in a big farm house a huge room & evendles, & settled ourselves in very comfy.

136

corrugation of mid deep
Pineapple.

wing's 6 long × 2-sh.ing 2½

The next day was perfect, & we basked until the Divisional came round, & went with him & Division to see about Bde. Details, we had 2 days rations, after which apparently no arrangements had been made, the beastly staff misgoverning. We should ration from our Butts 12 miles away in Area 1. No M.O. either, so there were some jawren.

Yesterday 25th Johnson (2nd in command of one of the Tyneside Scottish) came round; he was Div? Detail Officer, absolutely useless & fearful cad, & began ordering me around so I chucked him; he replied in an Low-ishina, with form pages of "Garrison Orders" for a move to Ag (4 miles away down the Scarpe), to commence at 4.30 (it was then 3.30), so I jibbed, & sent back a snorter pointing out his moment-tardiness, no Transport, no rations until they arrived at 6 A.M. etc, & thought I could move 170 men to Ag without all this uproar, he responded most decently, & said I could move when I liked, but then in rolled Tozer Rye, the D.I.C. administrative man for Supply etc, & said "you don't have until tomorrow" so I showed him Johnson's Orders! It was fair wild. I met Hamm, a young Lieutenant in the A.S.C. He was originally in the 16th. It was unmilitated Lame, and came to the 3rd O.C.B. (If he was a Tommy) He was a nephew of Sullivan, & I had had the pleasure of shaking him affectionately. He was much improved, & we had a great jaw, & then I got some transport from him to shift to Ag with. The weather had turned bitterly cold again, & was very trying to us, we were soon in our beds.

Last day, perfect sunshine, went to Ag after lunch, only about three miles, settled ourselves in & such. We were again lucky in getting a good billet, & the faithful Gallegos cooked excellently. Kal Kendrick commanding the 11/Suffolks (an awfully good chap): he had been laid down with Malaria, an awful cross; took him & Havre dinner over a very nice fire, when we smoked in our kitchen.

telephone message came that a car was coming to take me to Divl S.A.A. beyond Blangy to take command of the 24th N.F. so had to be a Derby Car. arrived 10 minutes later & away Gillespie & I set, drove through Arras & up the Scarpe to Div. H.Q., found them all most affable, fixed with Hew & Whiskey, had a word with Richardson, who was very nice. soon to 102nd Bde H.Q., renewal acquaintance with Hem & Polesgride to take me to 103rd Bde H.Q., had a drink with 102nd & so on. Found Bde H.Q. in Oppy Line overlooking Chemical Works & Tampour, brof. 2 days dug outs. Before Brigadier Griffin, a Lancashire Fusilier regular, lost an eye, & day one ear, but great sportsman, who gave me a drink, by did time I was beginning to smell a rat that something unusual was on, & it was gently broken that we were pushing in the morning & 28th my Battalion be the right, leading the attack!!!! That to to! had a yarn & so down to B'n H.Q. about 2 a.m., damned cold, found the Batt'n in a sunken road, & H.Q. a little way in the side of it, all ready there were the acting 2nd in Command, Captain Downey, the Adj't, the M.O., & a sick subaltern (none rather windy), so we were close packed. However as it was cold it didn't matter, we had several alarms of gas in the night, but only puffs – the adjutant & I got in his mask, & we were glad when morning came.

A nice day though chilli one, spent the morning getting to know officers, & inspecting the situation, we were in a road leading from Tampoux roads, half way down the ridge, & got fairly shelled now & then; you could see the Appoon 57th Div. going about in sound all over the place, where they had copped machine gun fire in their attempt five days before, you had a magnificent view of the battlefield, & it didn't look over promising. had a brigade pow-wow at 12 noon & was introduced to the other Batt'n Comm'rs, one was Richardson, a 20th Hussar, who had been a subaltern doing musketry at Sandguard when I was there. The Brigadier had only taken over the day before, his former one having been sent home for since of concussion & commission on the git. (they certainly did nothing). I heard that my predecessor (who succeeded the C.O. killed

143

on the 9th, I had got had wind up, & had been out during the day before. After lunch Dowling took me down through Fampoux to the front line, a dirty place. Trenches only about 3ft deep, & a mix-up of a front line, like opposite.

Found Richardson (commanding 26th) in his H.Q. at E, just a shaft dug by the Bosch, & of course facing east, in commencing a dug-out, but better than nothing. Found a large group of about F where the rations were changed each night, so agreed to plant half the Batt? there prior to the attack. Back to sunken road & explained ideas to the Co. Commanders & their sub. alterns. There were no Question Orders of any description from Bde or Div., except the barrage table & objectives, & no Batt? orders — it was just a "go as you please".

Had an excellent dinner, & then commenced the Relief of the Front Line at 9 p.m. The adjutant & the sick absentee told half Davis had went, with wind vertical, & I never saw the former again. The 9th hotly shelled going through Fampoux, & when H.Q. went up about midnight, the place was in an awful mess, whereas when we went up in the afternoon, it was quite tidy & nice. The shelling delayed things, & we had not completed Relief until 2 a.m. It was a pistol 7P. in the night, as Rupert Co which was only some 150 yds from the Bosch, took ages relieving. Our H.Q. trench running through E was just packed, with my H.Q., the H.Q. of the 26th & 1 Batt? of the 27th who were going over in close support to us, so till Richardson shifted out of his shaft, I sat on top with Dowling & Gillespie: it was quite impossible in the trenches.

At 2 a.m. I went round the line, withdrew all troops from BC & dumped them in the quarry, which was r. comfy, on the eastern lip, so that they got a fair start in a sharp retreat on the Chemical Works. Others weren't much noise, & very little firing, & hardly any Verey lights. Seen that the Capt. Ralf were ready at A-B, & then retired to my H.Q. to await the show. Found the 27th very noisy, & full of rum, so ejected

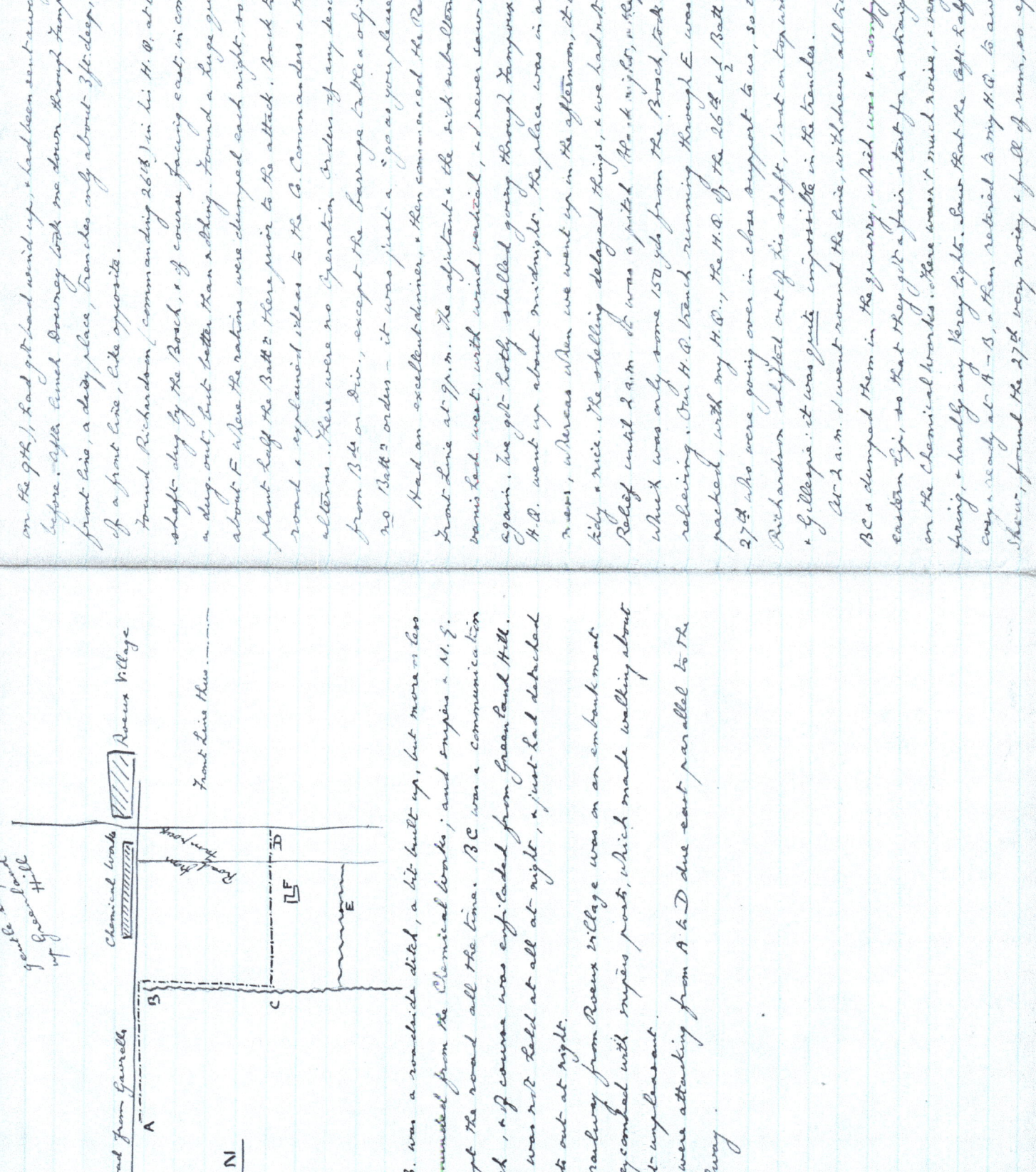

Road from Gavrelle
A — B, Chemical Works, Roeux Village
Front Line thus ——
Railway
C — D
E
N ↓
gentle slope up of Greenland Hill

A.B. was a roadside ditch, a bit built up, but more or less commanded from the Chemical Works, and snipers & M.G. swept the road all the time. BC was a communication trench, & of course was enfiladed from Greenland Hill. C D was not held at all at night, & just had detached posts out at night.

The railway from Roeux village was on an embankment & honeycombed with snipers posts, which made walking about most unpleasant.

We were attacking from A to D due east parallel to the railway.

144

It was darker than on the 9th, & there was a mist on, and it was most eerie standing on the edge of the quarry, & seeing the men only when there was an extra near shell burst, and when they were on the edge of the barrage they were just like folk watching a fire. The 27 & 8 were most comic; they went out by dribs & drabs & very slow — I was in front of them — & when the Boche barrage came down, they clumped & ran about like rabbits just one way & then another. I don't think many of them got past the quarry, but slid peacefully into shell holes where they stayed until dusk.

145

them from the noise of shell round my H.Q., & hurled my own H.Q. out of the scrimmage.

Zero at 4.25 — a heavy barrage on the chemical works, but the machine guns were in front of them. I went on top to see the show. Stationary we had a wonderful overhead machine gun barrage. The noise of which lasted us immensely — it sounded like thousands of whips cracked in the best hunting style. He could only see by the glare of the barrage, but our men went well out of the quarry & seemed to get well & easily under the barrage; & then the Bosh barrage came down; it wasn't at all nice coming back from the quarry to H.Q. The 27th were very funny; they came out in dribs and drabs, & as the shells burst, these small groups ran to one another & formed larger ones & they looked just like Irishmen at a Race Meeting.

When daylight really came, we couldn't see a soul. The Chemical works had been badly shelt, but that was about all, & our men were apparently holding on about 50 yds short of the works. Could get no answer by runners, so sent a Cpl up to find out; he came back with the comforting news that all the Officers were casualties! So I sent Downey up to straighten things up. The men in front of the Chemical works would of course have to stick until dark, but he wanted to find out how A-13 had got on. Lt Andrews, a gunner F.O.O. went with Downey, by giving a big roll of telephone wire. They got it across the viaduct — the sniping & M.G. was torrid down the road — & formed our line strung out in shell holes just east of the road, & then Downey got hit, snipped through the hand, along the side of it. Lt Andrews had the telephone fixed up, so I went up myself — found at foot of the 27th shell in the bank running through E, lying in cubby holes in the side of the bank, picked them out with my revolver & chased them over the top. A sniper was very busy in the railway embankment & nearly got me several times, so I sent two of my stalwart escort to fix him up, & they came back with his helmet, rifle, bandolier, and bayonet. It was a very nasty job crossing the road, apparently no one had had the sense to dig it up, so I set some men on to dig trenches. (I had already had two runners killed there,) by evening we had a sheltered crossing dug. Meanwhile we had to run the gauntlet of M.G. fire from the Chemical Works, & weren't too long in nipping across. I found things in Joseph's scheme 93 th. rather a ripping our men. They were in the Boche front line, sand as it was, just a line of shell-holes joined up & of course there is no glory. However I found Mr Andrews & got hold of a sergeant. Poor Downey was badly hit, part of the skull, but we could not get him across the road – it was much to dangerous. He laid a stretcher bearer with him & was half unconscious & obviously sick. I wandered along with the Sergt & found all the men asleep!! So trusted them up. May 11 When so consolidation was there were no officers & practically four N.C.O.'s. they'd lost all initiative, so I put them on making strong points of shell-holes (there was plenty of choice of those & bags of sandbags). It was most unpleasant as the Boche was in every shell-hole, & had been penned by our barrage. When lifted only lifted. One had gone close in the nearest shell-holes from where he was sniping at anything he saw, & we had like jolly nippy dodging across the trenches bits. We joined up with the 25th on our left, & I met many of their battalions who said their line extended up the hill a bit, but ended in the air, as the division next to us hadn't been able to leave their trenches, to our line was something as opposite. We had a chat in a capacious shell hole, & I gave him a drink. His men having got beyond the front line were stung out in shell-holes and the Boche ditto, sniping one another, so we were worse off than we were, as they couldn't shift. They hadn't seen anyone from behind so I was of load of news. I thought I had better be getting back, when our guns began shelling Greenland Hill on our left, & we saw the Boche running down the hill towards the left of the 25th. The guns gave them beautifully & the left

By the 25th gave them a warm reception, & finally of the few anxious minutes they faded away into shell-holes, & all was quiet again.

I thought I'd better get back, as if they counted our lot, they would want some moral support, so crawled, jumped, & ran till I was fairly in safety, & to back to the road crossing. That was very nasty as the M.G. was making continuous bursts along the road, & the bullets were spitting up the dust most uncomfortably. The men though R had worked well, & it was no longer a case of laboriously climbing up into the road, as they had they side-steps up, one good got across right quick, still — it was no use sitting & looking at it, so I up & ran across & took a flying jump into the trench on the other side, tell my women and Neudecen to come across when things were quiet, but the Scout-Cadets came over at once, & we returned to my H.Q. collected all the rifles & ammunition they could & made themselves comfy. There was a tree-covered bend, & we made a decent firestep, and sandbagged our flanks, so that we could straighten up a counter-attack. One my signallers had been over to the granary, to which there was no track, & had drifted back very calm & ends he couldn't find, so we had quite a nice mob of about 20. We had no Lewis or machine gun, but stacks of ammunition. There were no men in the part called "original front line", all the remnants of A & B Co being moved down in shell-holes between the jumping off place & the chemical works, who couldn't shift until dusk. Whether there were any left one couldn't tell, as it was quite peaceful there except for M.G. bursts from amongst the chemical works. Whilst I had been away a wounded Officer (through the wrist) had run in and gone down to be dressed: he had a dollop of yarn, apparently, A & B had been met by M.G.s as soon as the barrage lifted, & had caught it pretty considerably in the neck, & accordingly on very little help from them. Luckily our aeroplane with Brigade was interested, so I could put them wise, & held long talk with

---

[Sketch map showing: D Road C at top; Chemical works, Sniping post, A Road B, Granary, Jumping Off place, Strong Point, H.Q., 36ing Point, Skin]

13 Officers

C.O. } at H.Q.
Signalling Officer

1 wounded in wrist       A
couldn't move
1 " up in the Road   D.
D°     1 Sowerby
3 reported killed in front and
couldn't get no news of them

Leaving 5 Officers unaccounted for
1 A
2 B
2 C

the Brigadier & told him just what had seen, he was greatly relieved, as the other Bde HQ knew nothing & apparently had taken no steps to find out.

It was rather funny how I got my Bde HQ so far forward. The line (25 A 127 A) had chosen me; it was only a little there was in a hand about 500 yds behind me; it was only a trench covered in, in fact "something" but before my arrival, so I couldn't find any place. He suggested jogging in with them, but they said "no room". The only other place was an unfinished Bde HQ in the same trench, which I inspected & found was covered with a waterproof sheet!! Which didn't appeal to me. There was nowhere else, & the Bde had 4 pm me chosen to start, at the prov: 10 Bn Rebel at 4 pm & knowing the but an Rachis ever been any Bn there not even & knowing the waterproof sheet, I said I'd let him know later.

My HQ was exceptionally far forward, but I had telephone communication with Brigade, & really the other were much better back, & had even attack been successful. Besides which it appeared most probable that the trench K-L in which were the 26th & would get an awful hammering, much more than the forward area, & so I decided to take over the one I did, & had great difficulty in persuading the Brigadier to allow it. He did get command silently stalled, but we missed all the Certain they put down on K-L at zero, & again when the counter attacks were coming off. They didn't seem able to find exactly where my trench was, of course it was only a short length, but I only had two dozen with it during the whole day, though any amount just short in over.

Whilst I was talking to the Brigadier, he told me a Col. Mr someone or Nicholson, the Divl General had just arrived, so I had to tell it all again to him; he was rather vexed that I had seen to the front line, but I apprised him when I told him how all my officers were non est, & he asked most solicitously after my comfort, & promised to relieve my battalion at dusk at which we were all very bucked.

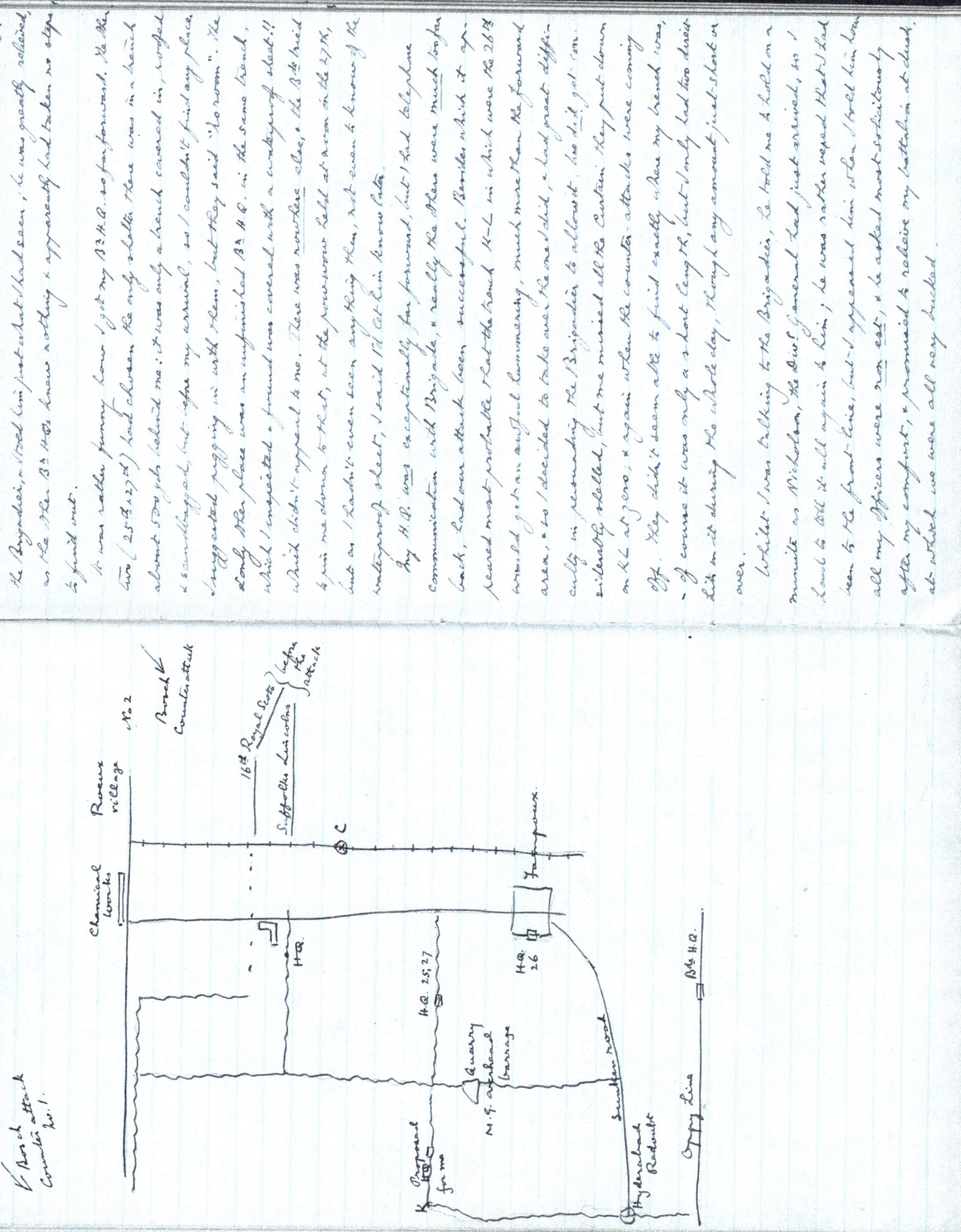

↓ 1st attack counter atk No. 1

The 16th Royal Scots went over at 5am on my right. A.C. on the right pushed resolutely into Roeux village. B.C. was held up next the railway. C. pushed on after A. but was held up by M.G. from Prospect Wood. Their right rear, and never reached the village. The Suffolks who were in close support, should have come along and swept the outfit into the village, but they funked it & never caught up C. & D., but went dogg-o into shell-holes, & Knife. There was much bad blood over this. As A.C. was next to a man, Lyon, & David being captured & Dalgety & another killed; half the company was killed, & the remainder captured. Stephens roundly accused Jack who was commanding the Suffolks that day (vice Kendrick sent to Acy Brick) of cowardice. Brown of C. Company was killed, Jordan & Standing wounded, & also from 18th were in a desperate plight. We heard from Lyon afterwards from Germany, and he said they'd right amongst the ruins of the village, & had they had some more push behind them would have Roll'd it; as it was, the Boche shot them off piecemeal until Lyon out of pity surrendered. They hadn't a dog's chance & wounded & would all have been shot

but then McLellan, my signalling officer, shouted for me to come up, no stop, I dashed, & had a real good view of a Boche counter attack from across the railway out of Prospect Wood. The railway runs along an embankment, but Prospect Wood was on a rise, & you could see the Boche streaming down the hill in great numbers, then our guns opened on them, rather late & most of the shells fell behind them, & to me anyways the attack disappeared behind the embankment railway, by 21 Brigade was behind the railway, the 16th Royal Scots holding the line, with the Suffolks & Lincolns in close support & the 15th R Royal Scots in reserve. Here was a culvert through the railway & C. & if they came on, it looked as if they would come straight through this & cut us off badly. So I told McLellan to phone Brigade, & ask for some of the 26th to be sent up to line the road-way, in case they broke through the 101st, & I proceeded to man our little fort, through this alas, was a contingency I had not counted on, and we should be shooting in the rear, with the Boche machine guns pelting us in the back – very pleasant idea. As a matter of fact, they broke through into the Communication Trench of the 101st, & the O.C. Lincolns shouted to Stephenson (command 16th "Royal Scots") that the Boche were in his hand sch. Stephenson said "Nonsense" & then "By God they are" & collected his remnants of H.Q. & proceeded to bomb them out. The Boche didn't like our certain gunfire on the slope, & at the same time didn't like Stephenson's bombs, & hesitated to go somewhere, & pelted back up the rise to where he started from, & very few got back. If you would see them going up pretty tight. Our carriage though too late for the initial counter attack fairly caught the reinforcements, & prevented them coming along to push on the good work, & finished that affair which we decided to leave alone, & only the Boche rolled the line of the 28th very heavily for about an hour to show his anger.

We had a very funny incident after this. McAndrew & I were

down at the right end of our trench, and McAndrew retired for a minute, down came a shell, & blew him clean out of the cill de sac into the main trench, shirt-tails flying. You've never seen anything so funny & I fair shouted with laughter. McAndrew was quite cross & could not see the joke a bit, & it made him more cross, to hear me sniggering to myself. He had a cigarette & then retired saying "Well I'm quite safe, seeing that the safest place is the crater made by the last shell", but alas! I was the exception, for & McAndrew's huge delight, up came the shell, & out flew with shirt-tails flying, & landed at McAndrew's feet. Mc. fairly shrieked with laughter, & I thought I'd never stop, & I couldn't see the joke & cursed him for a died ass, but he laughed the more.

McLachlan, my signal Cpl. officer, was a very amusing lad, & in the bottom of the trench hour after hour — he had never would up — & never shifted except to go down to the dug-out, & lean well & try every flaw, as he was scared a Bosch shell would go straight into it; being a Bosch shaft, the entrance faced the chemical works. He was marvellous looked awfully wonderful all day, & was quite useless.

I only had two visitors. One journey I made y₁ Co & R.S.M 2/₇ᵗʰ who came along to see if I knew anything, & being a sportsman/journal in the hunt for the sniper who worried, I got him a Belgian medal for it; the Brigadier, a week later, sent for me and demanded a name for the Belgian order of the Crown — apparently no one would have it, it had a nasty dirty plum coloured ribbon, & I certainly didn't; there was only McLachlan & I'd have thought himself an awful hero if I'd given it to him, so I got it for Steele, & he never forgave me; always used to be throwing it in my face. He was in command ? A Co of the 2/₇ᵗʰ when I commanded Him, & was an exceeding stout lad. He then went was of the 2/₆ᵗʰ, attached ₂/₇ᵗʰ, & Lieuᵗ with the 16ᵗʰ R.S. on my right. He had some fearsome journeys, but was wonderfully cheery, & always gay, & willing to go anywhere I wanted him.

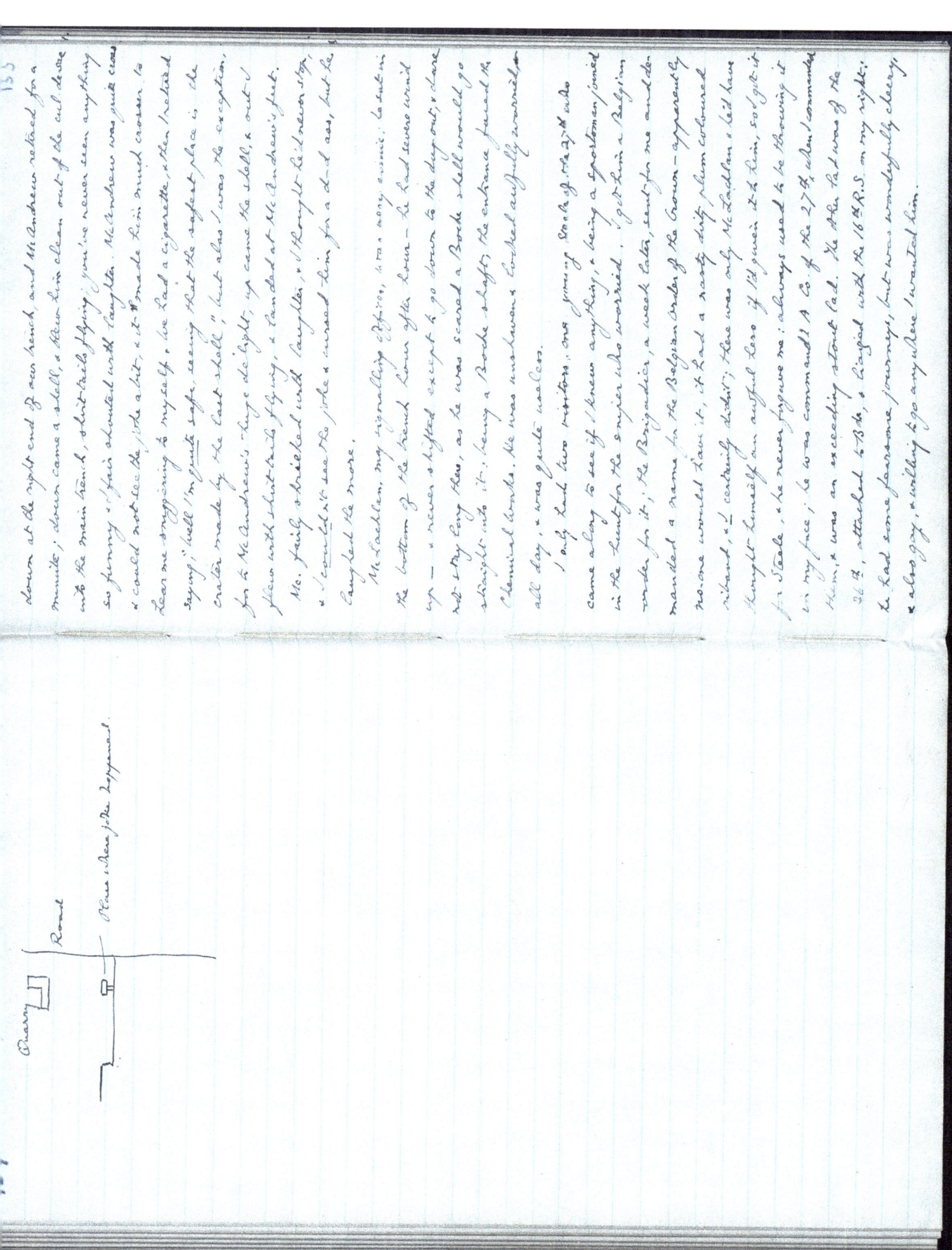

At 6.20 Richardson & his adjutant came up to relieve me, and his Batt? I had a rotten time getting up, the Boche could not help spotting them, as the trenches were mostly much too shallow, & you were wandering about exposed to the waist. The old Field R.C.T.s most unmercifully, & I was not a bit anxious to go out, however it was getting dark, so I wandered back across the top, & down the road to Tampoux — the road being exceptionally busy with the C.T.s on one left, & got there quite comfily. I met the 8th Batt. full of Cléopé, left word with Richardson to pass the word round for all my stragglers &c to rendezvous at our old Company place & Ammoned. Called in at our Aid Post at the east end of Fam-poux, it had had an awful trying [?], and what had been nearly untouched mansion in the 27th, was now pretty well ruined. Luckily the Aid Post was in the cellar, & well-shored up. I thanked for it several times during the day, as the Boche was knocking corners off it. A CO. of wounded of the 101st & our brigade were put on lighters behind the aid-post, & towed up the Scarpe nearly to Arras, but the damned man got a direct hit on one lighter, & nearly sopped some more, so they discontinued.

I found my machine officer very weary but very cheery, he was tired from Zeal to first, as most of the 26th wounded had been through him. He had had a good many of mine too, & was pre-pared for another rush when darkness came on & they arose from their shell holes. Dorney came down on a stretcher leavers back whilst I was there. He was very sick & livid & only left conscious, & the M.O. got a stretcher & sent him off right away.

I then g?d into the trench where the B.H.Q. of the 2½th & 27th was & joined them there; found them very shaken & jumpy, so much so that they ordered me leastly for lighting a cigarette, saying the Boche would see it. Such nonsense! I had had tons of late the Boch rained big shells onto our trench, & hit everything but hit the shelter; bursts in the ground outside each entrance over & over & all round; & finally made the ground shake. & I was sorry I was called in the kept on for a full hour, & then it dwindled away, & with it.

I had arranged to meet my H.Q. after dark in a little sand about 300 yds on off the main trench, so set off, but no one couldn't get along; it was a very narrow trench full of dead & wounded, & men lying flat who daren't move, so Gillespie & I took to the top again & got completely lost; we wandered round & finally Gillespie fell into a trench nearly on top of McLachlan, he was wild to see us. nearly hysterical & thought we had been knocked out; he had managed some rations from somewhere & a jar of rum, so we all partook & felt much better.

Then began to count the damage.. it looked pretty rotten on a first effort; one officer left, 13 & 17 D. & goodness knows what else of anything. I had had a day full of adventure, & had taken for myself one big dent in the helmet from Hy.1 Syphlos or Shrapnel which knocked me endways but did no damage except a headache, one graze on forehead which bled like a pig, but was only superficial (due to my foolish but unavoidable habit of wearing my hair cut on the back of my head, & (?) & (?) the nap-plain days; I had to wear it on the back of my head!), a bump on the back of my hand from a spent bit of shrapnel & very sore ribs, where a stone from a shell burst had hit me, one bullet through my collar, and one through 2 the waist of my tunic, so I had something to remember the Spurs by.

28 April

It was bitterly cold that night, & what with that, & the fact that the shells I was on, they got strictly contrary to orders from the trench side, was only 4 ft long, x 2 ft. high, & the excitement, I didn't sleep much, & was glad when dawn came.

29th

Live rations & back to our own trench road, many men showing to find out what had blown in during the night, not one of my subalterns being taken down on a stretcher with three bullets in him, but wonderfully cheerful, found quite a nice party there when 1 g.R. in, but the casualties were very heavy: 3 officers killed, 8 wounded, & 150 N.C.O.s

& men, killed, wounded, & missing, so it was with a sad heart I wandered up to Brigade for a pow wow at 9 am. The Brigadier was naturally rather upset at such a start for his effort as a Brigadier, when he heard our reports, but we got to business. Temple commanding the 27th, & Surry commanding the 25th knew nothing of the events of the day; I don't think they'd slept out of their blooming shelter from Zero till the morning after; Richardson of course being in Tampoux. Likewise knew a thing. So the Brigadier asked me to write out a report, & commented rather caustically on the fact that only 1 C.O. could give him any help, or knew anything of what any of the three battalions had been doing.

29th

He had a good dinner in the sunken road; the men were dog tired, but quite cheery & at 5 p.m. we all moved up into the Oppy line, the last real line the Boche had with dug outs re; real good ones. The M.O. came up about 4 p.m. and said that most of the wounded were lightly hit, & though we couldn't get the exact total, it looked like about 40 killed & missing & 110 wrounded. Another cold night, but Mac the Quartermaster arrived up with a Lewarack full of groceries from Arras, & we dined gorgeously on the fat of the land and rum — just McLellan, the M.O., myself & the D.A.M.R. Rest

30th

day were a perfect spring day, not a cloud, quite warm, sitting in the big wide trenches in the sun out of the wind; saw numerous air-fights, & three of our machines downed by a marvellously quick, seemingly painless Boche search, & very little shown. Rest day try. Had a perfect view of the battlefield which was perfectly peaceful, hardly a shell over, about certainly no hate, & it looked ridiculously simple just to collect & mot & march on the Channel looks at

31st

9 p.m. we marched out & were relieved by the 1st Division, who were the next on the list, & who by the way, came to grief just in a similar manner, & shung out the battle eleven atter picked no up at Atthis, & transport the battu elevens at an

oil factory just east of St Nicholas, where our Colonel B mat- no, and 2 captains & 3 subalterns, who took over rooms to the company of the remnant. McKenna took me to a big house in St Nicholas, the eastern suburb of Arras, where I had a gorgeous fire, a big feed, & we tucked in & devoured what was till midnight. When I retired to a very comfy bed in a bedroom with a fire in, & slept like a top until 7 a.m.

When I went up to see the battalion, they were much better after a good night's sleep, and were busy & having a washing. So handed them over to the Senior Captain with orders to be at the entraining point on the Lille Road at 2.30 p.m. — then the doctor, Padre & I went to Arras, had a gorgeous bath, & then to the Hotel Commerce for a real good, a regular oun- ashes on all the dainties of the land. I had seen Stephenson in the morning, he was very glum, & had lost about half a [Brown?], [Lyon?], Henderson, Duff, Dalgety & Mackenzie, all good except Duff, the whole of A Company & a percentage of B & C. Whilst we were at breakfast in our billet, there was a great air fight. Strijker overhead & we dashed out to see it; finally a Boche plane came circling down in a spinning nose dive, amidst huge applause; everyone thought it was scuppered, but - within a 100 ft of the ground it straightened out & landed perfectly in some bare land within 100 yards of our billet. The Bosche Lord up & the swine up, & came down on the only way out. But the battalion and embussed at 3 p.m. & had a very pleasant drive to Grand Rollacourt; arrived there about 5 p.m. The country was looking perfectly lovely in the sunshine, & the village was quite un- touched & looked a paradise in our eyes. Very nice billets for officers & men, & a just out wet women & Pujol, when they were all comfily in.

Rest-day; spent seeing that all the men & animals were comfy, & that rations were O.K. wonderful what a time it took, as of course fine weapons lots of billets for the

Head had a narrow escape on the night of the 27th. He brought up rations through Frampoux (no picnic that night either) up the road past the quarry which leads bang into the Chemical Works. He was guiding the column and absent-mindedly never noticed it (it was a very dark night) & meandered solemnly on till he and his circus arrived at our isolated posts strung across well to the front of the quarry. They were somewhat surprised to see him & he had an awful job extricating himself without any more noise than possible, & was jolly glad when he found himself back at the quarry safely.

companies, billets for all the specialists, the signallers, Lewis gunners, bombers, & B.H.Q. Transport. Cooking of course was done in the field kitchens, an animal like a double water cart, which is capable of cooking a meal, & real well, on the march. When you arrive in billets, you just run it into the farmyard, up by the roadside, & dish out the meal. They are a magnificent invention. Of course in places where you stop, you build ovens of bricks & clay, & indulge in wild orgies of fancy cooking. It was a perfectly heavenly spring day, & after the struggles of the month, it was paradise to have no shelling on, & to know that they couldn't put the much prayed-for "Morning hate" gas stuff & rifle grenades & rifle shots & refreshments.

My Echelon B consisted of the Commander, a butler of the late adjutant, 1 subaltern whom I made a Co. Commander, a stalwart man, & most useful, also infantry ditto, 1 subaltern. He had who had gone out the night before the attack. I took this company away from him on the spot. Wasn't a bit clean. He had been Brigade mulator, taking up rations to all Batts on pack mules, an excellent job. From Rhodesia, a great pal of his late C.O., killed on April 9th. Had formerly belonged to King Edward's Horse. I gave him the other company, & he was excellent. My two nominees both turned out first-class. The adjutant's truth was no great shakes, and so was CC. the fourth captain, had been muddler Helped Robins out up to the 28th shows, he wasn't much good either. This left me McLachlan whom I was forced to make adjutant pro tem; he was no good as a company commander for the moment there was never all the officers I had, & when & damned hard adjutants I had to do it. Thanks myself, & I was pretty full up, specially as none seemed to have a nominal roll of the Batt?, and I had to start right from the beginning. I just sent who no had, who we ought to have, & whom we might expect. It was a big day, but I was jolly fit after two nights good rest sleep, & one got to know a lot about the lot & that way. Had a Zeppelin's orderly room staff, & sacked the lot when the new drafts came up.

Next day was another find one, were started parades and sorting out: work: an awful job with such new arrivals. However small the company (you must keep your platoon to it, & however small the platoon, it must be divided up into sections). When one had subdivided a company into 16th, you would find some sections consisted of one man. Wickham, the R.S.M. gently came round whilst we were having lunch, and was most complimentary, & said I had amply justified his selection (I cannot afterwards there were great heart burnings amongst the other 2nd in Commands that I had been selected after only two months as 2nd in Command of A Batt'n in France!) and altogether was most kind. a Ring ret a table with Div¹ Commanders. I went over to see the 16th Royal Scots (6th M.G. units away) at Lui St Roger, had Tea at B⁴ H.Q, went to the Company messes, & to bed by gun.

The next two days were repeated & rested, or rather the Coy did. I was full of office work, checking casualties, writing to missing Officer's relations, and recommending G.O., applying from the return of officers from courses, writing to signers unduly absent Officers on courses (every one), looking Company & Battalion rolls, besides the 100 routine letters per brigade.

writing up the War Diary, which apparently had not been touched since the 5th April. However! That was a job of type also; only one officer had been in the G. O. Show, & they knew nothing of officers had been in the 5th April. He had a Church Parade on Sunday, at which we turned out quite smart, as he had a bit of new clothing - the men were simply falling to pieces & were only held together by safety pins.

On Monday we set out for Bonguemaison, only a small lot of six miles, & as we meandered off early we were

A. Company                                3rd Noy

No. 1 Platoon    No. 2 Platoon    Lieut. 3 P.    No. 4 Platoon

No. 1 Section   No. 2.    No. 3    No. 4.

We went into the line some 400 strong; ten 150 casualties leaves us 250. Take away Transport, Signallers, B⁴ H.Q. leaves say 170. which is 42 per company (20) Each platoon 10 men (at the outside for Co. H.Q had a some out of that), leaving an average of 2 men per section! The sections were 1. Riflemen.
3. Bombers (Hand)
2. Rifle grenadiers
4. Lewis gunners.

Afterwards they did away with the rifleman and made 2 Lewis gunner sections. Rifle bombers & riflemen made one Lewis company, as the rifle grenadiers used special rifles which were not accurate for marksmanship, and Lewis gunners & hand bombers the other half. 4th & 5th men

168

lunch, was to dinner with B.Co. of the 16th R.S. had a very cheery evening, & rode home about 11 p.m. The colonel, Stephenson, arrived back from Amiens about 10 p.m. just as I was calling in at Bn H.Q.: he was in great form; he & Kendrick had been feeding well, & he was most amusing. Evans who did so well on the 9th in the front of the line with me, has got his majority, & is 2nd in Command — a good man, & finally, captured by the Bosch in his dug-out in April (1918).
Some of them came over to tea with me next day —
Rawson, killed at Passchendaele, Evans wounded & captured at Passchendaele & Hearne, captured April 19; had a very cheery tea, and cocktails before their departure, at full galop at 7.30 p.m.

Whitty, whom I had made Co. Commdr., contrived that duty with bombing Officer, & we were up firing live drills. one man, deathly scared & refused to handle them. till Whitty threatened to tie one round his neck & pull the pin out, when he thought better of it. The bomb explodes five seconds after the pin is pulled out.

169

well there by lunch time, the cookers carrying on with the cooking en route. Billetted the men down & round dinners, & then landed at my billet, a real old Chateau, a bed with a canopy to it, in fact quite splendid. It was cold marching, but in a nice walled garden we slept away the afternoon in the sunshine. Next day, May 6th, we marched to Montelet, some 5 miles. it rained a piece, but was nice & cool, & we got there, after dinner on the round, about 3 p.m. We marched across down country & then dipped deeply down to Montelet, right at the bottom of a very steep narrow valley, a straggly village. Got em all billetted in, & reported to Brigade that billets were full, & no to tea. I was billetted on the mayor, a cheery old ruffian, who would persist in talking to me in very rapid French, & he was a nuisance, for whenever he saw me, he used to button-hole & walk with me, thinking it a great honor to Robert with a live Colonel.

That week we started training. I was draft joined us on the 9th, & filled us up again; the men knew very little. So we started from the beginning, & had a week's platoon training. Then on 14th started company training, & then they got excited & said we must start brigade training on 21st — ridiculous as men are very ignorant of the rudiments of war, and don't even know any drill. However as the Div! man is going to inspect us shortly, we must per-form. We started open warfare stunts on the stack of course by batts in an own training ground, a big expanse of land up on the downs. I thought them turned bad, but Brig. de was quite pleased. I thought I expected too much. We had magnificent weather. Left as the douce & brill. at sunshine, the men bucked up no end at it, & cooked very heartily & cheery.
Horrified by news that Bn! man, giving & inspect us on the 25th, however no was getting worried; & will help all they can. My Company Commanders are pretty commanded, & will help all they can.
We were lucky in having just ds the 27th a conference, and

founded up on the downs, formed the up by 9 a.m. We were nearly late on the Brigade Major. Luckily the least idea how to put out markers for us to march on, & when we got on them, the line of the two battalions was like a dog's hind leg, & it took a long time to straighten them out. The men panted very much & bad man, which gave us a good start, after which the Div¹ men suggested Battalion Drill!! which I hadn't heard of since 1891!! However Le Cerne off with two easy movements, when I told him, & we scrambled through. Then we lay about whilst 27ᴿ were inspected. The Second in Command was taking them as Temple the C.O. was on leave. He was an awfully nice Regular, badly wounded in 1914 at Ypres, but as he had been in hospital ever since, he was rather rusty.

Then we moved off and I did a Tactical Scheme, an attack, the 27ᵗʰ in front, then my Battⁿ came through them & proceeded with the second phase of the attack. I had impressed my Company Commanders that they must push along without me, as I should be right out of the way, & Watt and Whitty put some pep. into it, & worked jolly well. When we were moving up in waves, the men got the jumps, & the Batt⁵ looked like one wide mob at a race meeting, but I galloped around & straightened them out before they came in view of the gilded staff, who were engaged watching the 27ᵗʰ starting the attack, and everything went on beautifully afterwards, & we pushed along & got quite a good position without getting clubbed together, to rest when the bag C their 'cease fire', it looked quite nice. It was a deuced hot day, & I was dripping, as I had heard that things were rather at a standstill one at one time, and had chased up to hustle them, but found when I arrived that they had got a move on again.

We had a four word all sitting along a bankside, with the brass hats in front. Div¹ Gen¹. expressed great satisfaction, & said he'd found much more knowledge and

172

Temple was a temporary Lt-Col., whereas I was only Acting, & the real C.O. of the 27th was in England, and might come back, whereas he of the 27th had been killed, so it was only fair that Temple should have the permanency, and had the C.O. of the 27th come back, he would have taken over from Temple, & Temple would have become supernumerary.

173

initiative than he had expected, that batt. commanders had apparently been instructing their Co Commanders on the right lines, &c. &c.

So we broke off & lunched with Brit. Staff. Plan the 25th & 26th were inspected; i.e. of the 27th & 24th had to do enquiries which consisted in galloping around a searching masses of men to scatter, & lunatics standing about doing nothing to do something, under cover of telling them that they were under M.G. fire from such a place. They really were shocking, & in a temper Ld. Div. sounded the 'Cease fire', long before the close of the operation. At the poor woun. ta. asked no two unmasked wires what we had to say, & ungracefully said nothing. Whereupon Ld. Himself to the officers of the 25th & 28th & said "Well, I have", & started up braiding them in unmeasured words, so I came away, & went & had a smoke. I believe he slaughtered them absolutely.

We didn't finish till 5.30 p.m. & rode home in the cool of the evening, sunburnt to the bone & as dry as a rock. Temple & came & drank a bottle of wine with me, wild Scotch; it was topful & cool off the ice, under the care of the M.O., & then we felt better.

Last day got orders to take over the 27th & was rather cross, for I had worked hard & got the 24th in some order, & had got to know everyone in so doing, whereas I should have to start all over again with the 27th.

On Monday, May 28th, got orders to shift up to Arras again, & Cpt. Cardan at 6 a.m., had a beautiful cool journey & we marched out to our old camp at St Nicholas where we were in Divl Reserve. Last day we moved up to a ravine half a mile behind the railway, just south of Bois de Maison Blanche, had a beautiful Bivde concert sleep out, I am H.Q. 28, & the men in quite good mes quite close to.

28th & May 17 contd. Got on in the beautiful camp, luckily in entered our area, so we had B^n H.Q. alongside it, with a farm with a bath beneath it, & told my in dabar there in great style. The camp I was just about in the old No Man's Land, or rather No Man's Land passed through it, & as only portions of it had been levelled up, it was a fair death trap at night, except towards Arras, what with trenches, shell holes & wire, strewn– Had I refused point blank to move out at night, except to– wards Arras, & even then always had a trusty guide to meet me at the roadside, for no lights were allowed & all night long you would hear depressing voices calling for the Tyneside Scottish, 24th M.T. & so on, from men hopelessly lost in the mix-up of camps & debris. Our horse lines were about a mile away, in fact the whole division had theirs there, & they used to get frequently bombed at. Luckily the bomb choppers were either very good shots, or our luck was in, for they never put one nearer than the road, half-way from us to the lines. They did considerable damage there though, & bagged many mules & horses.

Next day, after a heavy night's rain we moved about 3 miles north, to a ravine looking towards over Belfaid, the Blue Line, on railway line of the Vimy-Arras railway. quite a nice cozy place with a magnificent concrete dug out for B.H.Q. & underneath this were the signallers & Headquarters Officers. The concrete dug-out was only so by name, as, built into the side of the ravine, it was level with the ground, & you walked straight out on to the floor of the ravine. Headlees they, it was in the western side of the valley, so the loons found the Boche, but the ravine was so narrow that it would have blown your tactics & chaps into it. We have dwelt in one sketchy [arrow] dug out

—— after settling in, I went off in search of Billy, as I had been some of the RND about. Spent

9/2-17. But horse lines which were on the ridge behind

177

our old Rocincourt position, a place in those days continually swept with M.G. fire, & there was shown where the R.N.D. guns were. This was on the west edge of the Vimy ridge, just north of where we took it on the 9th April. It was a perfect day, & as I was in no hurry I walked across our line of advance, which was perfectly dry now, & only cleared at the roads. Then from the Bois de la Haven Blanche I climbed M.E. & found the guns in a nice cosy spot just under the toe of the ridge. One got a beautiful view of the old battlefield, & it was very curious to see the crowds of mules & horses all lined up, & men & transport leisurely wandering up the roads, which in olden days were just lines of shell craters, only marked out by the stumps of the trees on each side of the road. The guns were very good, and I was escorted around until at my gun I met a man who knew where Billy was, at D.A.C. at Anzin. Anzin was a village in the Scarpe valley some three miles behind Arras, but too far to go that afternoon.

Next day after lunch I had my horse up, & rode down to Anzin & soon ran Billy to earth, in lines on the bank of the Scarpe, quite a nice place & plenty of trees & wild flowers & Billy looking like a prize-fighter, so fat & burnt. We had a long yarn, & then Lin Adjutant gave him half a day's leave for next day, & I rode back via Arras in the cool of the evening, very peaceful, only an occasional shell dropping at odd places, as if even the gunners were bored, & ours were just asleep, & very little noise from over the ridge. I rode up & treated the graves of Fott & Hanborn who were buried in a small cemetery just below the Bois de la M.B., very carefully tended, & so back to own ravine.

Billy arrived in time for lunch on Thursday 3/5/18 & Kay, & I had indeed a special decent feast for him.

179

The lads in the Rose were very nice & tom conjured dishy
hers at being in Tommy's clothes, after lunch he & I strolled
onto the hill above, & lay in the sun & swapped yarns of
our experiences. It was just lovely basking in the sun and
warmth. We had tea, then wandered up to our battlefield,
& showed him round, after which we dined, & he left about
8.30 p.m.

Friday 1st of June. I went up to inspect the line we were
taking over. It was on the western edge of Greenland Hill,
of frightful memory. It always reminded me of the Battle
Orders indoors, when Douai was given as the final objective!
Our line started half a mile south of Gavrelle, where we
joined onto the R.N.D. Pen Gavrelle was a lump of red
rubble, which every five minutes was stirred up by a
Boche shell, why Goodness only knows, as no one ever
went there in daylight. Our way to the line lay over the
level crossing, south of our Blue Line, up to the Point du Jour,
which was the highest point of that part of the ridge, &
you had a lovely view of Arras, & also right east to Vimy,
" with Douai still our final objective. It was a plain
enduring that month of Greenland Hill which was really
isolated & an offshoot of the ridge, north of the real one,
above Roeux village. Then you descended the east-side of
the ridge, not on the road thank you! but down the open
hillside, & came to the old Boche line last line of trenches
before he took to the open & dug himself in on the first
slopes of Greenland Hill. From this line, which was our
Bn H.Q. Line, the ground again sloped down, as bare as
your hand, and our front line was just on the first rise
to the hill, the Boche as normal having the overlook of us.
The dip between B.H.Q. and the front line was the devil
as any rain that came flooded into it & waterlogged
the communication trenches, whilst our front line received
all the wet from Greenland Hill. The 2/4 were in then,

the 16th R.S. rest on their right, so I went along & saw Stephenson, & found them all very fit. Though still very cross with the Lindsey & Suffolks near the place of R. 28th April. The B'H.Q. being Ger- man was very strong and well built, & the dugout entered had been brought round sideways, so that they didn't offer a target for bodes shells. Got back for lunch – a grilly evening – and in the evening we meandered from our ravine to the railway cutting just south of the level crossing of the 9th April. It was just a rubble heap of chalk, and the shelters were all on the west bank of the cutting. B'n H.Q. was there, & of course had g'd themselves well sand-bagged in, but our gunners were stoutly beamed with a covering of chalk, & the men were in burrows all over the east side of the cutting.

Next day we remained there; there were two 60 pounders in the valley just behind us, which made an infernal noise. Otherwise it was very nice & beautifully fine, though they shelled us some at night.

Sunday was another perfect day, & we still remained in the cutting, quite happy, as any move meant the front line & jolly little peace and rest.

I meandered up again on the Monday, & went round the front line, quite a simple bit, but the devil's getting there, as a thunderstorm had simply romped off the chalkland, & filled the C.T.s just-to-one's tummy, & the mud at the bottom was very claggy. The front line too was stampish, & as there were no shelters for the men & very cramped quarters for the Officers I'm afraid they'll have a thin time.

The line is grateful just quite a sharp N piece from where we join the RND with one very unfortunate Craoure which had been blown in, & only a piece 2 foot high tunnelled under it, & as the water was some six inches deep, communication was awkward, & one generally about over the top & in again, until I got it cut through. About 30 yards beyond this, the trench struck off nearly at right angles, too, & dwindled away to nothing. They said the Boche stalled it to glory, & we finally gave up digging it out, and left a gap some 40 yards in our line. Instead of the next batt'n coming up to the gap, we had a company beyond it completely isolated from the other bit except at night, when if you liked you could dodge the M.G.s which continually played on it, & save yourself nearly a mile and a half of a walk.

We took over that night starting 10.30. Relay complete 2.20 a.m. Brouldon Burnett very jumpy for fear his men wouldn't get away before daylight & Lane 2 climb up to the Point de l'Iron murder, stall fairs, however I think he'd just do it. It was so light even at night, that one had very little spare time in which to relieve, though after the initial effort of course it didn't take so long.

Tuesday 5th. Settled down in the line. Went round after lunch. The water had gone down, but still was up to your knees, so I dispensed with mine, as I had the day before, & dwelt in shirt sleeves — mud forward & my self. Men very cheery & officers ditto. Apparently quite happy & settled down again. It was a long job going round so that is nearly of up towards our right made it a round about journey. I was pretty weary when I got back. Brrrooom, my adjutant, sleeps like a log, & even to one the telephone, so when I am in at night I take over the telephone as being simpler than having to waken him every time. Brownjetha's yarns of the visiting questions asked by Brigade at all hours of the night are quite true, & they get some pretty snuffy answers from me if anything were unimportant. I take a note off & say I'll see about it, but there are very few of those, mostly them being trivial things which could quite well have waited.